Liberty *and* Laissez-Faire

Liberty
and
Laissez-
A Primer on Freedom, Government, and Prosperity
Faire
Steven Soderlind

Archway Publishing books may be ordered through booksellers or by contacting:

Archway Publishing
1663 Liberty Drive
Bloomington, IN 47403
www.archwaypublishing.com
1 (888) 242-5904

Interior Image Credit: Special Collections Research Center, University of Chicago Library.

ISBN: 978-1-4808-4404-9 (sc)
ISBN: 978-1-4808-4403-2 (hc)
ISBN: 978-1-4808-4405-6 (e)

Library of Congress Control Number: 2017903875

Print information available on the last page.

Archway Publishing rev. date: 3/29/2017

Dedication:
To the rising generation

CONTENTS

PREFACE

This book invites readers to examine the relationship between liberty and laissez-faire against a backdrop of calls for less government intervention. As a primer, it introduces fundamental concepts and invites readers to think and decide for themselves.

Approaching liberty as a goal and government as a means, the discussion will emphasize social and historical context in the relationship between liberty and the size of government. It will incorporate the ideas of eminent economists and political thinkers, both advocates and critics of laissez-faire. In particular it will reflect on works by Adam Smith, John Stuart Mill, Friedrich Hayek, and Milton Friedman on the one hand, and Thomas Malthus, Karl Marx, John Steinbeck, and Thorstein Veblen on the other. Many readers will be surprised at the points of agreement and disagreement, left standing on grounds that readers are better served with unanswered questions than unquestioned answers. Wisdom often resides amidst competing dispositions.

The rising administration has indicated strongly that it will shake the foundations of public policy "to make America great again." Hopefully this little book will help set the stage for a productive episode of shaping and pruning. Best not to throw out the baby with its bath water.

In the end, all social institutions - including government and markets - operate in a constitutional setting, subject to agreed authority and procedures. Constitutions and charters provide the key mechanisms for managing the dynamic fit of government with liberty and prosperity.

May this book prove useful in our pursuit of "a more perfect Union."

Steven Soderlind
Apple Valley, Minnesota
December 2016

INTRODUCTION

"I want government that is so small I can barely see it."
Rand Paul, 2016 presidential candidate

Hardy libertarians promote freedom and self-determination. They resent oppression, including slavery, abusive oversight, intrusive government, unwarranted discrimination, muscular opportunism, and confining ideology.

These days, especially in America, the "libertarian view" is tied to an optimistic vision of reduced government and free, unregulated markets, traditionally called laissez-faire. Proponents from Raul Ryan to Rush Limbaugh claim to have distilled this practical stand from respected economists, referencing the likes of Adam Smith, John Stuart Mill, Frederick Hayek, and Milton Friedman. They also take heart from astute reflections on Soviet communism associated with Ayn Rand, William Buckley, Jr., and Patrick Buchanan, to name a few.

So the matter for many is settled: liberty and laissez-faire complement and reinforce one another. But make no mistake, laissez-faire can also undermine liberty by tacitly condoning an oppressive status quo: human trafficking, racial and gender discrimination, monopoly, religious chauvinism, etc. Many see The

Great Recession as a consequence of deregulation – toying with laissez-faire.[1] Thus a deeper examination seems in order.

The goal of this essay is to provide a relatively balanced account of connections between liberty and laissez-faire. It will highlight the views of eminent economists like Smith, Hayek, and Friedman, and add venerable critiques associated with Malthus, Mill, Marx, Veblen, and others. Many readers will be surprised at the complexities involved; even strident supporters of laissez-faire have harbored reservations.

A primer, this essay offers only an introduction. It surveys a vast territory, spotting grand features and encouraging deeper investigation. Hopefully readers will appreciate both the portrait and the prompts.

---

[1] The Great Recession, 2007-2011, brought carnage mounting to several trillion dollars in foreclosures, business setbacks, lost jobs, bank failures, and debt, not to mention non-monetized confusion, heartache, and depression. It followed an era in America of opportunistic, prodigal, even corrupt behavior by unfettered lenders, borrowers, bundlers, and developers, which in turn followed financial deregulation under the Financial Services Modernization Act of 1999. Moreover, while hundreds of American banks were shuttered between 2008 and 2011, not a single Canadian bank failed, the Canadians having resisted deregulation. All told, America's Great Recession might warn of laissez-faire as a threat to liberty and prosperity.

CHAPTER 1

In a Nutshell

Laissez-faire, "leave things alone," generally disparages government intervention. It imagines a social milieu in which individuals and households operate without interference, hence the connection from less government to liberty. Left alone, individuals in their various circumstances can choose what to buy or do, when, where, how much, and with whom - as they see fit. Without governmental restrictions, laissez-faire seems to promote liberty and market prosperity.

Meanwhile we occupy a world of oppressive circumstances and predicaments: slavery, intimidation, overlords, xenophobia, persecution, monopoly, racial oppression, sexism, criminality, contaminated water, etc. Against that backdrop, laissez-faire can be an avenue of acceptance, complicity, and even support for the status quo, hardly the vanguard of liberty. How can we envision such complexity?

Figure 1 offers a Venn diagram of the social universe with two dichotomies: liberty versus coercion and laissez-faire versus government intervention. Liberty is portrayed as a circle, laissez-faire as an ellipse. The circle and the ellipse overlap, their intersection being "Liberty and Laissez-Faire," our title.

Figure 1.

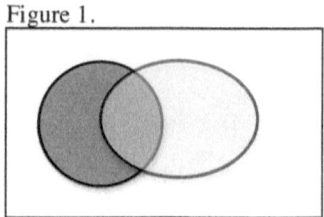

Thus we imagine four categories of social circumstance:

- liberty and laissez-faire (medium gray),
- liberty and not laissez-faire (dark gray),
- not liberty and laissez-faire (light gray), and
- not liberty and not laissez-faire (white).

Consider the examples in Table 1.

Table 1.

Category	Examples
Liberty and Laissez-Faire (Medium Gray):	A farmer's produce stand with customers, picking a TV show, browsing the menu at a restaurant, legalized heroin
Liberty & Not Laissez-Faire (Dark Gray)	Emancipation Proclamation, Voting Rights Act, equal opportunity laws, Bill of Rights (freedoms of speech, assembly, etc.)
Not Liberty and Laissez-Faire (Light Gray)	Slavery, ethnic or religious persecution/discrimination, traditional restraints on women paralysis at birth or due to accident or illness
Not Liberty and Not Laissez-Faire (White)	Imprisonment, Jim Crow ordinances, environmental and financial regulation, mandatory vaccination

These assignments are discussable. Placing the Bill of Rights in the category of "Liberty and Not Laissez-Faire," for example, appreciates that constitutional government came first, then the Bill of Rights to be enforced by that government.[2] One might also challenge whether legalized heroin, toying with dangerous addiction, belongs in the category of "Liberty and Laissez-Faire." The rationale here is that legalization would remove a governmental restriction to allow free choice by adults.

It is easy to imagine more ambiguous situations, like following a boss's orders (light gray or medium gray?), consumer protection (white or dark gray?), or buying meat subjected to mandatory federal inspection (dark gray?). Situations can be murky.

Systemic oppression, like racism or sexism, raises the question whether laissez-faire or government action constitutes the better course toward greater liberty. Among those who advocate laissez-faire, some will argue that a particular pattern of coercion is not sufficiently nasty to justify intervention, the cure being worse than the problem. Others will acknowledge unwelcome power and injustice, but argue that laissez-faire promotes social processes that will eventually overcome oppression. Milton Friedman represented this view in *Capitalism and Freedom*. To wit,

> I believe strongly that the color of a man's skin or the religion of his parents is, by itself, no reason to treat him differently; that a man would be judged by what he is and what he does and not by these external characteristics. I deplore what seem to me the prejudice and narrowness of outlook of those whose tastes differ from mine in this respect and I think the less of them for it. But in a society based on free discussion, the appropriate recourse

---

[2] The Bill of Rights was passed in 1791, three years after ratification of the Constitution. Massachusetts continued with its established Congregational Church until 1833, now seen as an instance of federal patience.

> is for me to seek to persuade them that their tastes
> are bad and that they should change their views
> and their behavior, not to use coercive power to
> enforce my tastes and my attitudes on others.[3]

Thus Friedman counseled patience and open discussion to deal with racial and religious bigotry.

Impatient with this approach, social activists point to enduring patterns of oppression for which hands-off policies and respectful discussions have not borne fruit. Laissez-faire to them abets established oppression and coercion: white supremacy, sexism, ageism, homophobia, family violence, and police brutality. If liberty enjoys priority, how long must people wait for progressive dispositions to take hold?

Friedman imagined free markets as a vanguard of liberty, taking heart in what he called "unanimity and nonconformity."[4] He also argued that racial and gender oppression might succumb to the liberating influence of impersonal markets, as it had for Jews in anti-Semitic Europe.[5] Though he was personally opposed to racial and religious discrimination, Friedman preferred not to "use coercive power to enforce my tastes and attitudes on others." But as history unfolded, the Civil Rights Act of 1964 came just two years

---

[3] Friedman, Milton, *Capitalism and Freedom* (Chicago: Chicago University Press, 1962), 111. Earlier in the book Friedman had written of economic freedoms promoting political freedoms. "Economic arrangements play a dual role in the promotion of a free society. On the one hand, freedom in economic arrangements is itself a component of freedom broadly understood, so economic freedom is an end in itself. In the second place, economic freedom is also an indispensable means toward the achievement of political freedom." 8.

[4] The key notion of "unanimity and nonconformity" anchored the discussion in chapter 2 of *Capitalism and Freedom*, "The Role of Government in a Free Society." The term corresponds roughly to liberty and laissez-faire or "medium gray" in our Venn diagram.

[5] "The preservation of Jews through the Middle Ages was possible because of the existence of a market sector in which they could operate and maintain themselves despite official persecution." Friedman, *Capitalism and Freedom*, 108.

after *Capitalism and Freedom*, acknowledgment that America's foundation of white male supremacy persisted stubbornly in spite of market forces and open debate. The nagging question was whether a white person would willingly change places with a person of color in the United States even fifty years hence.[6]

To a libertarian, the balance of genuine social gain comes with reduced oppression. But even with the intervention of executive orders, laws, and court rulings, the fight for harmonious liberty (the "medium gray" kind) remains an uphill battle. Racism, sexism, religious chauvinism, etc., are deeply rooted, resilient features of complex society. To the extent that people gain pleasure or profit from oppressing others, expect resistance to "political correctness." Change will come slowly, the "dark gray" increment of liberty being tarnished by the coercive imposition of government. In this sense the Confederate flag often emerges in protest of "political correctness" that marches under the American flag with constitutional accreditation.

Thus we come to the heart of the matter: is laissez-faire or government action the preferred route to liberty? Relative to our Venn diagram, the "Circle of Liberty" can grow in its medium gray realm of "Laissez-Faire" or in its dark gray realm of "Not Laissez-Faire." That is, liberty can expand with growing brotherhood among racial or religious groups (medium gray), or liberty can expand with anti-discrimination laws, court decisions, and executive orders (dark gray). Proponents of liberty must wonder about dark gray, appreciating that the success of intervention will depend on cultural and historical circumstances, including tolerance.

In a nutshell, given its high priority, how should liberty grow

---

[6] The Civil Rights Act was passed in 1964, followed in 1965 by the Voting Rights Act. As citizens explored racism, many considered whether they would comfortably trade places with others in their society. This thought experiment helped somewhat in identifying oppression and clarifying prospects for progressive liberty, but the nation proceeded with caution, aware of Niebuhr's famous Serenity Prayer. To wit, "God, grant me the serenity to accept the things I cannot change, the courage to change the things I can, and the wisdom to know the difference."

and prosper? If gains in liberty seem barred in laissez-faire, should they be cultivated, imposed, or legislated into "Liberty and Not Laissez-Faire?"[7] Both laissez-faire and government intervention can expand liberty, but both can also trample it. Thus we confront the Yin and Yang of libertarian aspiration.

---

[7] Expect resistance to "political correctness" when government imposes liberty on a resistant public. Resentment can find expression by votes, flags, burned effigies, and insurgency. Meanwhile, traditional oppression simply morphs into new forms; old voting restrictions (poll taxes, arbitrary quizzes, and intimidation) resolve into less offensive voter suppression (somewhat burdensome proofs of citizenship, for example), and "separate but equal" (Plessy v Ferguson) resolves to a combination of private schools and passably resourced public schools.

CHAPTER 2

Liberty, an Evolving Priority

> A free man is he that in those things which
> by his strength and wit he is able to do is not
> hindered to do what he hath the will to do.
> - Thomas Hobbes, *Leviathan*

Liberty involves freedom from control by others. Its opposite (short of execution) is imprisonment and proximate predicaments like slavery, brutish oversight, unyielding dogma, confining custom, and abusive government. A more positive depiction of liberty denotes a social environment in which people manage their personal affairs according to free will and assume responsibility for their actions.[8] Importantly, liberty (dark gray and medium gray) enjoys a high priority in social philosophy and constitutional law, medium gray preferred.

Classical liberty faced two enemies: abusive monarchy and

---

[8] The concept of liberty arises only in social context and is distinct from independence because actions under liberty often impact others. Ancient appeals for liberty arise in Homer and Exodus. Today's association of liberty with rights, though more empirical, remains ambiguous, such as when one's right to swing confronts another's right not to be hit. So it goes with correlative rights and duties in liberty.

lawless anarchy. Searching for solutions, ancient Greek city-states adopted rule by citizens. Under agreed procedures, the citizens of fifth-century BCE Sparta and Athens convened routinely to legislate, administer, and litigate, confident that citizen input could countervail abusive or arbitrary power. In that context, Aristotle extolled the virtue of "magnificence," whereby the wealthier citizens of Athens willingly built its acropolis, theaters, and expansive infrastructure. Less-wealthy citizens could not achieve magnificence, lacking sufficient funds, but they could attain the virtue of "liberality" (contributions to neighborhood) and support the community by participation, conforming to law, and raising healthy, respectable children.[9] The word *idiot* comes from those days, referring to a self-absorbed citizen who accepts the fruits of community but contributes little to it.

Romans coined the word *libertas* from which came English cognates like liberty and liberation - but they reserved *libertas* for themselves, thinking little of enslaving, oppressing, and lording over others. Liberty was a tribal value.

Enlightenment thinkers of the seventeenth and eighteenth centuries, notably John Locke, Jean Jacques Rousseau, and Thomas Jefferson, imagined a "state of nature" in which powerful brutes might rule by force - but not without violating the "natural rights" of those they oppressed. The idea of a social contract arose as philosophers imagined the clarification and protection of those natural rights, allowing liberty to ride higher in more enlightened jurisdictions.

It was easy in those days of absolute monarchy to imagine protection from abusive rulers. It was also easy to imagine protection from muscular neighbors, notorious for intimidation, takings, bullying, and opportunism. Finally it was easy to imagine coercive institutions, many upstart liberals having churches in mind, appreciating the power of religious dogma over a parishioner's

---

[9] See Aristotle, *Nicomachean Ethics*, especially Book IV, "Virtues Concerned with Money."

thoughts and actions. Most Enlightenment thinkers were disestablishmentarians, preferring that citizens be free to sort and pick religious stands for themselves. Meanwhile, markets were seen as a progressive frontier that matched nicely with freedom from king, guild, church, and traditions. A new era would be increasingly free of aristocratic rule, moralistic teaching, and coercive traditions.

Today we have considerable experience with social contracts (constitutions, charters, and basic laws), sadly including constitutional governments that have vandalized liberty. In spite of protective constitutional language, for example, the USSR, Nazi Germany, and Jim Crow America terrorized millions of innocent citizens.[10]

It was the prospect of oppression at the hand of one's community that inspired John Stuart Mill's *On Liberty*, pondering limits to social coercion over private citizens. Even democratic majorities were prospective oppressors. Mill famously argued against coercion upon a person except to protect others from harm.

> The only purpose for which power can be rightfully exercised over any member of a civilized community, against his will, is to prevent harm to others. His own good, either physical or moral, is not a sufficient warrant. He cannot rightfully be compelled to do or forbear because it will be better for him to do so, because it will make him happier, because, in the opinions of others, to do so would be wise or even right. These are good reasons for remonstrating with him, or reasoning with him, or persuading him, or entreating him, but not for

---

[10] Other examples of abusive government abound in the history of genocide, torture, bluster, lynching, fraud, and blackmail. Thucydides provides a classical reference on abusive authority in his report on the Melian episode when powerful Athens subjugated a tiny, non-insurgent neighbor during the fifth century BCE, killing everyone against the chance of their siding with an enemy. See Thucydides, *History of the Peloponnesian War*, Book V, "The Melian Dialogue."

> compelling him or visiting him with any evil in
> case he do otherwise.[11]

Nations today adhere more-or-less to constitutions and charters that promise to nurture liberty by establishing civil rights and protections. Among the freedoms most commonly espoused are freedoms of speech, assembly, and religion. To countervail various blights upon liberty - criminality, ignorance, discrimination, and intimidation - nations have promulgated criminal codes, public education, anti-discrimination laws, and police protection. Many nations, including the United States, have added the mandate that government pursue full employment, especially against the crush of cyclical downturns with widespread joblessness that can crimp personal freedom and flourishing.[12]

Recognizing that illness and accident pose threats of incapacitation and dependency, many cities, states, and nations have invented ways to provide health care or require health insurance. That said, it is worth pondering whether, for example, illiteracy, illness, blindness, or disability undermine liberty. If so, when might such conditions that establish a greater likelihood of control by others constitute a claim for liberty's sake upon public resources?[13]

The Declaration of Human Rights (1949) asserts a set of international rights that have attracted a degree of global acceptance:

---

[11] John Stuart Mill, *On Liberty* (Indianapolis: Hackett, 1978), 9.

[12] The Employment Act of 1946 mandates attention to full employment by the US federal government. This American innovation featured a host of leaders in the movement to reform and improve upon capitalism, including Woody Guthrie, John Steinbeck, and Harry Truman.

[13] In his book *Development as Freedom* (New York: Anchor Books, 1999), Amartya Sen explores this line of thought, proposing that economic development expands freedom and liberty versus what he calls "unfreedoms" associated with material deprivation and destitution. Tangentially, where rights have been extended to a widening circle of people for their protection and self-determination (e.g., the Americans with Disabilities Act of 1990), liberty arguably grew in its "Not Laissez-Faire" (dark gray) mode.

freedom from slavery, freedom from torture, etc.[14] The Millennium Development Goals build on related "rights" (to potable water, K-5 education, etc.), exemplifying the process of emerging freedoms at the global level, though one must appreciate the absence of global government *per se* to defend or enforce such rights.

Most public intellectuals of the twentieth century emphasized the priority for liberty in practical terms; witness Reinhold Niebuhr, Friedrich Hayek, Milton Friedman, William Buckley, Jr., Abraham Heschel, W.E.B. DuBois, and Martin Luther King, Jr. Perhaps the most extreme valuation of liberty came from philosopher John Rawls, who gave it lexicographic status over other goods, thus ranking increments of liberty above any material gain or cost. His admiring but cautious commentators, the likes of Kenneth Arrow, Arthur Okun, and A.K. Sen, have encouraged readers to ponder more carefully such an extraordinary valuation.[15]

Of note, while strongly favoring free markets and decentralized authority, Friedrich Hayek appreciated the compassion of liberals for progressive change. Some will be surprised that Hayek's concern for liberty led him to challenge conservatism, which could do little better that what it conserved. In his postscript to *Constitution of Liberty*, entitled "Why I am Not a Conservative," he wrote,

> Let me return, however, to the main point, which is the characteristic complacency of the conservative toward the action of established authority and his

---

[14] The Declaration of Human Rights espouses thirty rights, beginning with (1) the Right to Equality, (2) Freedom from Discrimination, (3) Right to Life, Liberty, Personal Security, (4) Freedom from Slavery, and (5) Freedom from Torture and Degrading Treatment.

[15] See Arrow (1973), Okun (1975), and Sen (2009). Rawls's valuation arose from a hypothetical constitutional convention with representatives in a condition called "original position," not knowing their situation in the society they were organizing. Ignorant of their own race, gender, religion, etc., these representatives would protect themselves against undo discrimination by establishing relevant protections. Thus Rawls derived his high priority for liberty.

prime concern that this authority be not weakened rather than that its power be kept within bounds. This is difficult to reconcile with the preservation of liberty. In general, it can probably be said that the conservative does not object to coercion or arbitrary power so long as it is used for what he regards as the right purposes.[16]

Hayek harbored some concern that conservatives might block liberty by the use of power to resist progressive cultural change. He strongly preferred medium gray to dark gray, so-to-speak, but sensed a conservative penchant to resist both progressive legislation and social accommodation.

Today, after centuries of experience with markets and constitutional government, a relatively nuanced wisdom has taken hold, namely that "the market has its place, and it should be kept in its place." Briefly, while market forces admirably favor efficiency and free choice, they can also trample other, higher priorities. The right to vote, for example, comes with the stricture that one should not buy or sell votes, as such transactions would demean the value of franchise by assigning it a price, franchise being a political prize, not a market prize. Similarly, though one can imagine mutual gain from a contract of unconditioned servitude, such agreements are not allowed – presumably again because such contracts demean freedom and liberty.[17]

Finally, a "liberal education" intends to prepare students for lives of freedom and self-determination. By that standard, students

---

[16] Friedrich Hayek, *Constitution of Liberty* (Chicago: University of Chicago Press, 1960), 401. Being a conservative does not imply working actively against coercion or oppression.

[17] Though prohibited by Thirteenth Amendment, "involuntary servitude" begs clarification of the term "involuntary." Slavery is clearly involuntary, but how about "coal town debtors" or the so-called "reserve clause" in professional baseball? The courts allowed the reserve clause, which became an issue as players organized into a bargaining union. It was through union activism that players won "free agency," allowing them to negotiate contracts with more than one team.

do well to study the skepticism of Socrates, the rhetoric of Cicero, the resolve of Galileo, the civic and scientific engagement of Benjamin Franklin, the vision of Adam Smith, the charity and clarity of John Stuart Mill, the militancy of George Washington, the nonviolence of Mahatma Gandhi, the fortitude of Frederick Douglass, etc. Such an education girds one with thoughtful references to parry demagogues, ideology, and dogma. Of course, a person may choose submission in the exercise of liberty and free choice.

CHAPTER 3

Numbers

What constitute prosperity, liberty, laissez-faire, and government? Can such abstractions be measured? If so, how much of each do we have?

The most common measure of prosperity is GDP per capita (average annual income in a nation). It is a fraught measure for many reasons: GDP does not count valuable nonmarket activities like raising your own children or fixing nutritious meals at home; meanwhile, it counts costs for criminal justice and medical care that grow with criminality and illness, each of which challenges genuine prosperity; and it excludes major aspects of flourishing like health, safety, and belonging.[18] Neither does it attend to the distribution of incomes. Nevertheless, GDP provides a standard measure of the market value of goods and services produced for sale in a given year, making it a viable measure of market activity. When decomposed by sources of income, sectors of production,

---

[18] Evaluating products merely in terms of revenues and jobs, GDP and employment statistics systematically overlook future costs of things like brittle bones, heart disease, diabetes, obesity, and disappointment. Ironically, those long-term costs will not be recorded as setbacks, but as gains in income to doctors, therapists, and nurses, among others. Such are the ambiguities of conventional measurements.

type of expenditure, etc., GDP becomes a starting point for deeper analyses of material gain.

Many have argued that a better measure of prosperity would combine GDP with measures of environmental quality, public health, education, and the distributions of income and wealth.[19] The Human Development Index (HDI), for example, combines measures of income, life expectancy, and educational achievement, reported by the United Nations annually for its member states.[20] Another well known metric, but of socio-economic discouragement, is Arthur Okun's famous Misery Index, summing a nation's unemployment and inflation rates; this index gained political notoriety when used by Ronald Reagan in the 1980 presidential campaign.

Similarly, liberty might be rendered by an index that combines absence of slavery, freedom of speech and religion, access to transportation, education, employment, and police protection; access to teachers, lawyers, political processes, grievance procedures, etc. For example, the CIRI Human Rights Data Project developed an index to measure the extent of human and civil rights enjoyed by residents of nations around the world.[21] Other measures of liberty include Freedom House scales of political and civil rights, Amnesty International's Index of Political Terror, and the US State

---

[19] See Joseph Sitglitz, Amartya Sen, and Jean-Paul Fitoussi, *Mismeasuring Our Lives: Why GDP Doesn't Add Up* (New York: The New Press, 2010) for a comprehensive review of economic performance and its measurement. Also see Herbert Gintis, "A Radical Analysis of Welfare Economics and Individual Development" (*Quarterly Journal of Economics* 86, no. 4, 1972) for a broader view of social flourishing.

[20] United Nations, "International Human Development Indicators," accessed December 2016 at http://hdr.undp.org/en/countries provides an interactive map showing various measures of human development for each nation. In 2015 the United States ranked 6th in GDP per capita and 8th in HDI.

[21] CIRI's web address, accessed in December 2016, is www.humanrightsdata.com. The index ranges from 0 to 30 with Luxembourg ranking highest (score = 30) in 2011 and Iran the lowest (score = 1). Related to such indexes, Eric Posner (2008) has argued for "welfare measures" to replace "rights logic" in assessing foreign aid effectiveness, rights being easy to assert but hard to measure.

Department's Political Terror Score. The goal of such estimates is to take the term Liberty from the metaphysical realm to the empirical and analytic.

Finally one can imagine an index to measure the degree or extent of laissez-faire in a region or nation. Several such measures have been developed, often using the term economic freedom in place of laissez-faire. For example, the Heritage Foundation and Wall Street Journal developed their Index of Economic Freedom, a measure of business freedom, trade freedom, government size, tax burdens, infringements on property rights, and so on. Calculating this index for 178 nations in 2016 resulted in a range of numbers from a high of 88.6 (Hong Kong) to a low of 2.3 (North Korea). Other such indexes have been put forward, including an index of indexes.

Using such operational definitions of liberty, prosperity, and laissez-faire, one can begin formal studies of estimation and correlation. For example, comparing ten nations according to GDP/capita, HDI, and more, we get the comparisons shown in Table 2.

Table 2. A sample of nations: GDP/cap, HDI, and scores from Freedom House, Heritage Foundation and Amnesty International

Nation	GDP/cap 2015 USD	HDI	Freedom House Index of Political Rights 2015	Heritage Index of Economic Freedom 2016	Amnesty Intl Political terror scale 2015
United States	56,100	.915	1	75.4	2
Norway	68,600	.944	1	70.8	1
Arab Emirates	67,200	.835	6	72.6	3
Switzerland	58,600	.930	1	81.0	1
Australia	47,600	.935	1	80.3	2
Denmark	45,700	.923	1	75.3	1
Canada	45,600	.913	1	78.0	1
Netherlands	49,600	.922	1	74.6	1
Russia	26,000	.798	6	50.6	3
China	14,300	.727	7	52.0	4

Sources: GDP/cap from CIA World Fact Book, Estimates using PPP.
At https://www.cia.gov/library/publications.
HDI from UN Human Development Report for 2014.
At http://hdr.undp.org/en/composite/HDI.
Freedom House, Freedom in the World 2015.
At www.freedomhouse.org, scale 1=most free, 8=least free.
Heritage Foundation, Index of Economic Freedom 2016.
At http://www.heritage.org/index/ranking.
Amnesty International, Political Terror Score 2015.
At www.politicalterrorscore.org, scale 1 = least terror, 5=most.

Yet other images can help in the investigation of prosperity and liberty. For example, a five-point "Star" might represent five attributes of importance to prosperity, giving a visual representation of their composite, each point of the star related to a corresponding average. Consider the following measures:

1. employment rate (North Point)
2. average income (East Point)
3. average level of education, main householder (SE Point)
4. % of wealth held by top 1% of wealth holders (SW Point)
5. number of doctors per 1000 population (West Point)

These data might apply to households, communities, states, or nations. For the sake of play, consider three towns and their three representative "stars" A, B, and C in Figure 2 below. Which to you seems best off? Are there circumstances (e.g., age, region, or health) that might affect your assessment? For example, what if Town A has excellent water but C has water with dangerously high levels of lead? Or what if town B also features an exorbitant crime rate? We must consider such extra conditions to address issues of ambiguity and relativity.

Figure 2.

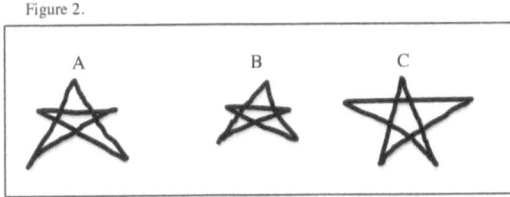

Analogous stars could be constructed to represent liberty, perhaps dimensioned as:

1. enforceable right to practice religion of choice
2. access to attorneys and courts
3. incidence of severe hunger

4.   access to elementary education
5.   likelihood of being a victim of crime

Other things equal, differently shapes "stars" invite assessment and discussion.

Related to laissez-faire is the size of government, which can be subjected to several measures. The United States has so many officially constituted governments with tax and spending authority that it publishes a Census of Governments every five years. The most recent census from 2012 shows the nation to have one federal government, fifty state governments, 3,031 counties, 35,879 municipalities and townships, 12,880 school districts, and 38,266 special districts (mainly soil and water conservation districts). That tallies to 90,056 different governments with departments and offices galore.

Employment provides another measure of government; America's single federal government employed about 2.8 million at full time in March 2012 with that month's payroll at about $17 billion. Meanwhile, the fifty states employed about 3.7 million at full time, with a cumulative monthly payroll of about $18 billion, while local governments employed 10.6 million at full time (another 3.3 million at part time) with a cumulative payroll of $46.6 Billion (plus $3.7 billion for part-timers).[22]

Another measure of government concerns expenditures. In 2016 the federal government spent an estimated $3.9 trillion, or about 21 percent of GDP, of which $.7 trillion went out as grants to lower levels of government. The states spent $1.6 trillion, and local governments accounted for $1.8 trillion. The sum total comes to about $6.6 trillion, or 35 percent of GDP, about the same share as was average in the 1980s.[23]

In relation to other nations, America's governmental share of national spending is relatively low. In 2014 Finland's government

---

[22] Data for March 2012 came from https://www.census.gov/govs/apes/historical_data_2012.html. Accessed December 2016.

[23] Data for 2016 came from http://www.usgovernmentspending.com/total_2016USrt_18rs5n. Accessed December 2016.

controlled 58.1 percent of GDP, Norway's share was 45.8 percent, Japan's was 42.1 percent, and Switzerland's stood at 33.7 percent.[24] Of course, public services vary among these nations, making comparisons difficult. Concerning education, for example, each of the other nations covers most if not all of a student's tuition for higher education and technical schooling, while the US covers only a small share of tuition expenses after high school. As of 2016 student debt in America amounted to almost $1.3 trillion, and the "average college graduate" in 2016 carried over $35,000 in loans.[25]

Of note, while government provides many services that enhance personal freedoms and liberty, most measures of economic freedom carry a bias against large government. For example, the Heritage Index of Economic Freedom penalizes for a larger size of government (measured as a share of GDP).

---

[24] Estimates from the Organization for Economic Cooperation and Development, accessed December 2016, https://data.oecd.org/gga/general-government-spending.htm.

[25] According to the Federal Reserve Bank of New York's "Quarterly Report on Household Debt and Credit," May 2016. Student debt ranked second among the debt categories in the United States, exceeded by only mortgage debt.

CHAPTER 4

Play to Discover

"Do not keep children to their studies by compulsion but by play."   –Plato

P lay enhances learning with engagement and enjoyment. To that end, consider again the Venn diagram from Chapter One with two dichotomies: liberty versus coercion and laissez-faire versus government intervention. Liberty was portrayed as bounded by a circle and laissez-faire by an ellipse. In the case of overlap we got four categories of social circumstance, neatly separated. That was our set-up, hopefully useful, though its simplicity naturally invites critical and thoughtful play.

In fact the world is hardly so clear-cut. Its inherent ambiguity calls for cloudy boundaries instead of tidy lines, and to that end we noted the case of a boss's orders at work; given a labor contract, the boss enjoys a right to rule and the employee bears a duty to obey. Is that liberty or coercion? Maybe 50-50? 60-40? It's ambiguous.

More examples abound. When a person's rights are newly declared but not enforced, is liberty enhanced? It is discussable, and it is ambiguous. Or imagine a salesperson answering a customer's question truthfully – but only out of fear for consequences that might follow a lie. The salesperson is to a degree coerced, her liberty bounded, perhaps in the customer's interest, and perhaps by government, somehow lurking.

Or imagine the circle sitting entirely inside the ellipse, Figure 3. Then there would be only three categories (no instance of "liberty and not laissez-faire").

Figure 3.

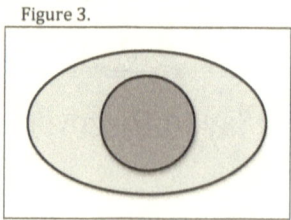

Why then would we want government? Of course, to protect rights or impose rules in the area of "not liberty and laissez-faire," which can be notorious for slavery, pogroms, arbitrary abuse, hate, discrimination, oppressive dogma, etc.

Cultural relativism can easily arise in assignments to such categories. Situations that would be considered unacceptably oppressive in Sweden might be standard and comfortable in the United States (where millions of people carry guns) or in Sudan (where women have acclimated to exclusion).

As for a correlate to the Venn diagram, one possibility is a four-pane window (Figure 4).

Figure 4.

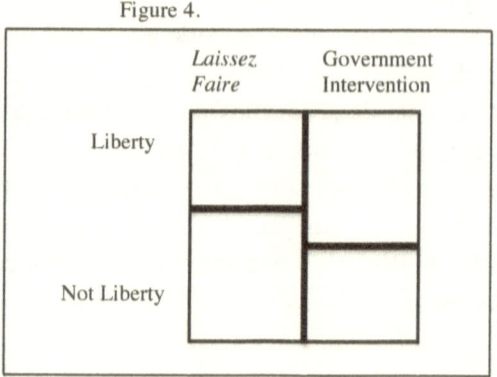

Again we have four categories, up to three of which might disappear. For example, the absence of government leaves just two panes. Given four panes, a new civil rights law, other things equal, might be recorded as more intervention and more liberty, represented by a larger upper-right pane. Perhaps some color-coding could reflect the intensity of pushback by those who previously enjoyed the power to oppress, suddenly taken. Maybe the pane showing Government and Liberty could be colored white in the case where there is little resentment, but red in the case of armed insurrection. A spectrum from white to blazing red could serve to represent intermediate outcomes. One might proceed similarly to represent and discuss environmental regulation, legalized abortion, or immigration reform.

Consequential events would resize the panes, change the colors, and bring time into the picture. Imagine a snake emerging in time, its momentary cross sections being rectangular with color-coded panes. How might you represent a riot following a Supreme Court ruling? Such is the territory of play.

In an earlier era, the likes of Adam Smith and David Hume envisioned the decline of monarchy and religion with the ascent of laissez-faire. Smith argued in that context that most of the gains in freedom would be in the area of liberty and laissez-faire.

Another correlate to the Venn diagram might arise by setting the two polarities into an orthogonal relationship. This portrait would take the form of four quadrants with coordinates representing intensities (Figure 5).

Figure 5.

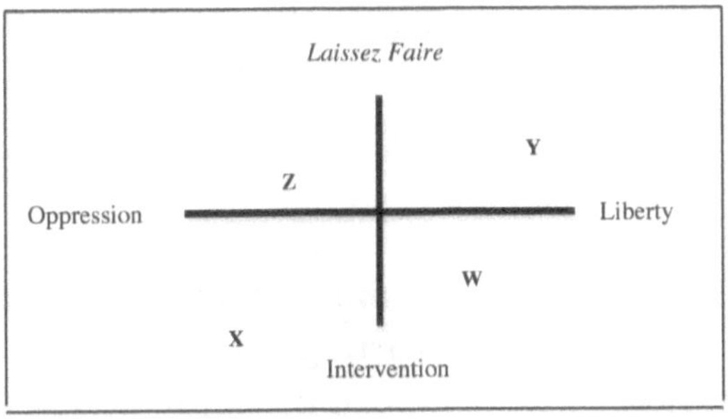

An African-American male facing oppressive "Jim Crow" ordinances could be represented as a point in the quadrant of Oppression and Intervention, say X, the location revealing both qualitative and quantitative information. Appreciating intensities, a more hostile version of "Jim Crow," perhaps with a meaner sheriff having deputized a surly mob, would be represented by an point farther down and to the left (representing more oppression and greater official intervention). Everyday racism, without sheriff or deputies, might show as points in the Laissez-faire and Oppression quadrant, say point Z.

Similarly, "a stop at the farmers' market" might be represented in the quadrant of Liberty and Laissez-faire, perhaps at Y. The Voting Rights Act might show as a move from Z to W, and a sudden reduction in the reliability of protections for voting rights could be represented as a move leftward from W.

The orthogonal setup naturally invites thoughts of correlation. This essay simply notes observations in every quadrant. Given than human nature is notorious for greed and envy, laissez-faire is likely to include plenty of coercion and manipulation – both oppressive.

That said, the world has become increasingly interdependent with global convergence in language, products, and lifestyle. Many gains have been mutual, such as my happiness being tied to yours or that both sides can gain in trade. Indeed, my prosperity is increasingly tied to that of a person in China, and this expansion of interdependence might be seen as a global movement into the first quadrant, Liberty and Laissez-faire. Think about that.

Adam Smith contemplated such a global connection in his *Theory of Moral Sentiments* when imagining distant catastrophes. To wit,

> Let us suppose that the great empire of China, with all its myriads of inhabitants, was suddenly swallowed up by an earthquake, and let us consider how a man of humanity in Europe, who had

no sort of connexion with that part of the world, would be affected upon receiving intelligence of this dreadful calamity. He would, I imagine, first of all, express very strongly his sorrow for the misfortune of that unhappy people, he would make many melancholy reflections upon the precariousness of human life, and the vanity of all the labours of man, which could thus be annihilated in a moment. He would too, perhaps, if he was a man of speculation, enter into many reasonings concerning the effects which this disaster might produce upon the commerce of Europe, and the trade and business of the world in general. And when all this fine philosophy was over, when all these humane sentiments had been once fairly expressed, he would pursue his business or his pleasure, take his repose or his diversion, with the same ease and tranquillity, as if no such accident had happened.[26]

Things have changed, but perhaps not so much.

This brings us to another playground, economics. Classical economics arose in the Enlightenment with a characteristically secular attitude. The exemplars of progressive thought at the time included Locke, Rousseau, Hume, Jefferson, Franklin, Kant, Condorcet, and Voltaire – not to mention Smith - each pondering the concept of a natural social order. The basic idea was in the air at the time, taken from cosmology and physics where Copernicus, Galileo, and Newton had mounted a significant challenge to church teaching that the earth sat at the center of the universe, or at least at the center of the solar system. As the church teaching fell short in that contest, society became the next frontier.

Did society have a natural order? If so, were church teachings

---

[26] Adam Smith, *Theory of Moral Sentiments* (London: A. Millar, 1790), III, 1, 46.

as far off in social and moral terms as they were in cosmological terms? Classical economists strongly affirmed the natural social order, and each proceeded to conjure possible trajectories. The consensus was that freedom from monarchy and church would lead to greater prosperity, at least for a while.

CHAPTER 5

Liberty and Laissez-Faire in Classical Economics

A ttention to liberty has been a persistent feature of economics since its extraction from natural and moral philosophy beginning in the eighteenth century. Building on a radical vision of self-organizing systems, economics emerged with a focus on the long-term trajectory of a free society, beginning with optimism about laissez-faire prosperity.[27]

The term laissez-faire was used first by Francois Quesnay, friend of Adam Smith, to advocate free trade. The idea was to allow freedom of transaction between consenting, self-interested individuals or companies, even when they resided on either side of an international border. This idea stood in opposition to the conventional practice of regulating trade to protect a nation's treasury (of gold).

Adam Smith, founder of modern economics and titan of the Scottish Enlightenment, carried the argument along by attacking

---

[27] To survey the history of economic thought, see Robert Heilbroner, *The Worldly Philosophers,* 7th Ed., (New York: Simon & Schuster, 1995) or Robert Ekelund and Robert Hebert, *A History of Economic Theory and Method,* 5th Ed., (Long Grove, Illinois: Waveland, 2007). The call for freedom began in the days of unbridled monarchs and rules of inheritance that imposed serfdom, career, and austerity upon most people.

the so-called "mercantile system," then dominated by monarchy, church, and monopolies. Smith railed against the licenses, tax breaks, and privileges for producers, retailers, and merchants in that system. He sided instead with the nation's consumers. To wit,

> Consumption is the sole end and purpose of all production; and the interest of the producer ought to be attended to only so far as it may be necessary for promoting that of the consumer. This maxim is so perfectly self-evident that it would be absurd to attempt to prove it. But in the mercantile system, the interest of the consumer is almost constantly sacrificed to that of the producer.[28]

In place of the mercantile system Smith proposed the "system of natural liberty," a relatively spontaneous social order ruled by self-interested consumers attended by self-interested producers and suppliers. In brief, he advocated the ascent of competitive markets where profit-seeking producers would serve consumer appetites and where competition would squeeze hard on excessive profits. This relatively radical proposal celebrated profit and self-interest versus moralistic teachings against selfishness, greed, and acquisitiveness. Smith argued that greed and self-interest could encourage innovation, division of labor, and lower costs of production. Importantly too, when profits correlated with shortages, they encouraged more production exactly where it would be most demanded.

Smith suggested that sovereign consumers and a competitive

---

[28] Adam Smith, *Wealth of Nations* (London: Methuen & Co., Ltd., 1904), IV, 8, 49. The mercantilists had advocated for a large treasury (of gold), promulgating six pillars of policy: export much, import little, employ all resources, favor home production, encourage population growth, and keep wages down. A low wage was important to this system, as it kept costs down in the interest of international competitiveness.

market system would outperform their mercantile alternative with higher output, lower costs, and a more generous provisioning of the public. England under his "system of natural liberty" (or "perfect liberty") would never be a Utopia, but it would be materially better off than under mercantilism. The gains would build on expanding liberty, growing mainly in the laissez-faire intersection (medium gray) with the rise of markets.

Consumers would assume the lion's share of control over the economy, ruling by their free choices. Producers would follow.

> ... the obvious and simple *system of natural liberty* establishes itself of its own accord. Every man, as long as he does not violate the laws of justice, is left perfectly free to pursue his own interest his own way, and to bring both his industry and capital into competition with those of any other man, or order of men.[29]

As Professor of Moral Philosophy, Smith knew that consumers could be whimsical and wasteful – especially as their incomes rose – prone to misdirecting resources just as surely as had the kings, bishops, and moguls of the mercantile system.

> With the greater part of rich people, the chief enjoyment of riches consists in the parade of riches, which in their eyes is never so complete as when they appear to possess those decisive marks of opulence which nobody can possess but themselves. [30]

---

[29] Smith, *Wealth*, IV, 9, 51. Italics added.

[30] Smith, *Wealth*, I, 11, 83. Smith's less famous book from 1759, *Theory of Moral Sentiments*, examined the phenomena of human sympathy and ambition. In that work he discussed human morality and its corruption from a naturalist or secular point of view. One need only read his accounts of "foolish purchases" or the "poor man's son" ("whom heaven in its anger has visited with ambition")

He knew that consumers often would steer resources to ridiculous ends and excesses, but sensing net progress he emphasized the overriding virtues of a natural, self-regulating social order based on human nature and competition – guided by reasonably responsible consumers. People could act with a modicum of discipline and propriety, which seemed a good bet as kings and bishops receded from power.

Extending his progressive vision, Smith proposed many important roles for government, including national defense, public hygiene, highways, bridges, interest rate ceilings, public education, and taxes on luxuries and unsavory behavior. His "system of natural liberty" would thrive even more with good government. For example, he imagined that specialized labor would have a problem with torpor.

> The man whose whole life is spent in performing a few simple operations, of which the effects are perhaps always the same, or very nearly the same, has no occasion to exert his understanding or to exercise his invention in finding out expedients for removing difficulties which never occur. He naturally loses, therefore, the habit of such exertion, and generally becomes as stupid and ignorant as it is possible for a human creature to become.[31]

That said, Smith suggested that universal access to schooling would become a uniquely important investment for the nation's human resource.[32] He also saw government regulating the prod-

---

to appreciate the moral challenges faced by consumers and producers in his "system of natural liberty."

[31] Smith, *Wealth*, V, 1, 178.

[32] Universal access to education was a radical proposal at the time, what with enclosures and the rising class of wandering poor. "But though the common people cannot, in any civilized society be so well instructed as people of some rank and fortune, the most essential parts of education, however, to read, write,

igal instincts of bankers, lest the financial system suffer crises. Thus Smith saw government as a means to enhance a nation's wealth in his expanding "system of natural liberty." Education and monetary control would be part and parcel of the nation's growing wealth.

*   *   *   *   *

Smith's views gained favor in erudite circles and among profit seekers. A relatively virulent strain of his optimism went so far as to inspire sublime hopes among philosophical anarchists like William Godwin who speculated that even disease, anguish, and marriage might disappear with the dismantling of monarchy and religion.[33] What a fine world might lie ahead, he thought, if only Smith's vision would be allowed to mature, liberty and laissez-faire joined!

That hopeful narrative took a broadside with the arrival of Thomas Malthus, whose *Essay on Population* foresaw a nasty future for laissez-faire based on an exploding population that would test the earth's carrying capacity. As the population and its appetites grew exponentially while the supply of food grew only "arithmetically," Malthus envisioned a destiny of starvation, war, disease, and widespread subsistence. Suddenly laissez-faire held the prospect not of prosperity but of abject predicaments, including pestilence, disease, war, and hunger. This was hardly

---

and account, can be acquired at so early a period of life, that the greater part even of those who are to be bred to the lower occupations, have time to acquire them before they can be employed in those occupations. For a very small expence the publick can facilitate, can encourage, and can even impose upon almost the whole body of the people, the necessity of acquiring those most essential parts of education." Smith, *Wealth*, V, 1, 182. Smith devoted Book V of *Wealth* to the role of government.

[33] Godwin's radical views led to hearings in the Privy Council, an early instance when libertarians tried to disassociate from their close cousins, anarchists. If interested, see Godwin's *Political Justice* from 1793.

the optimistic vision of natural liberty projected by Adam Smith (Figure 6).

Figure 6.

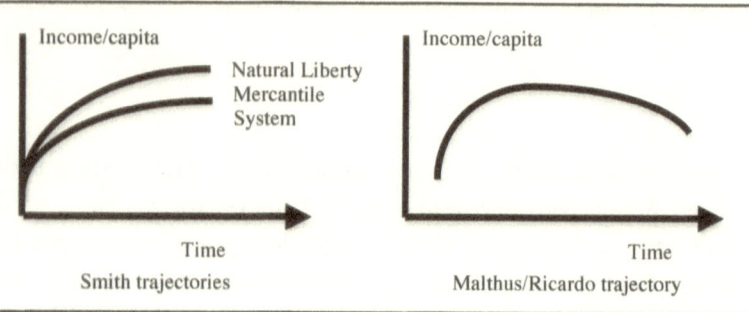

Malthus enjoyed the company of three influential friends: David Ricardo, James Mill, and Jeremy Bentham. This group of four entertained themselves with discussions on progressive legislation, free trade, and birth control. One can only imagine sparks flying among such brilliant combatants – Bentham espousing utilitarian progressivism, Ricardo strategizing against falling profits, and Malthus legitimizing the income of landlords – all within earshot of James Mill's very precocious son, famously educated under the tutelage of his father and Bentham.

Ricardo deepened the gloom that Malthus had spread over laissez-faire by adding injustice to the story. As a growing population forced ever more extended margins of cultivation, profits would invariably fall and hard-working business owners would eventually join hard-working laborers at bare subsistence. Meanwhile parasitic landlords would enjoy high rents and great wealth with little effort. This destiny could be but delayed with free trade and specialization. Such was the revised outcome for laissez-faire, and economics became The Dismal Science.

Smith, Malthus, and Ricardo offered only theoretical visions, simple and allegorical. None of the three anticipated the technological innovations to come, but each supported laissez-faire in the area of commerce. Free trade became the standard of economic thought. To be sure, government had its place in this economic vision, but it would be restrained to certain roles: defense, health and safety, monetary oversight, bank regulation, public education, and infrastructure – much as prescribed by Smith. Beyond such roles noninterference would be the rule, allowing social traditions to persist.

Regarding the plight of workers whose freedoms were severely crimped by poverty, classical economists stood more or less ambivalent. Smith, Ricardo, Malthus, and even Marx presumed a subsistence wage, often called "a crust of bread." Profits depended on the cost of that crust, which the worker got in any case, no matter its cost. Expensive wheat meant expensive bread, which cut into profits. Smith's metaphysical "natural wage" was basically that "crust of bread." Ricardo openly expected a subsistence wage, and Marx saw the subsistence wage not only as the proper payment for labor power, but also as ignition for social unrest and revolution.

Classical economics essentially retained the "utility of poverty" doctrine from the earlier mercantile era. Low wages were baked into the social order, supporting profit, and profit carried the hope of more jobs and continuing prosperity. Laissez-faire optimism thus channeled a traditional indifference toward labor – brutish and incorrigible. This has been part of the tradition, adjusted slightly in the event of scarcity; that is, certain specialties of labor might escape subsistence for as long as their scarcity persisted.

* * * * *

By 1850 John Stuart Mill, erstwhile precocious boy, had taken over as Britain's reigning political economist, writing on population, war, labor, value, ethics, and more. In 1848 he published the first edition of *Principles of Political Economy and Taxation* with its advocacy of laissez-faire for the realms of production and general commerce. Following in the classical tradition of Smith and Ricardo, Mill advocated free trade and the standard roles for government (defense, justice, infrastructure, public education, etc.), but with some additional twists, urging support for the abolition of slavery and the extension of women's rights. As to public finance, Mill came to favor a proportional income tax and heavy inheritance taxes, sensing inheritance as unearned, hence unjust.[34] Appreciating that it would take time to reform the system from its feudal tradition of inheritance and bequest, he wrote,

> With regard to inheritance, ..., I (have suggested) ... freedom of bequest as the general rule, but limited by two things: first that if there are descendants, who, being unable to provide for themselves, would become burthensome to the state, the equivalent of whatever the state would accord to them should be reserved from the property for their benefit: and secondly, that no one person should be permitted to acquire, by inheritance, more than that amount of a moderate independence.[35]

Mill's most famous essays were "On Liberty" (1859), a clarion call inspired by the threat of oppression from one's community, "On Utilitarianism" (1863), riffing on Bentham's positions from earlier days, and "On the Subjugation of Women" (1869), urging the extension of rights, protections, and franchise. While still holding to laissez-faire in commerce, he blasted away at abusive

---

[34] Inheritance raised issues of justice and liberty for Mill. Indeed, while slavery is association with race in the United States, Europeans knew it as a matter of class and inheritance. One was born to being a butcher, a baker, an aristocrat, or a slave, as the case might be.

[35] John Stuart Mill, *Principles of Political Economy with Some of their Applications to Social Philosophy* (Middlesex, England: Penguin Books, 1970), 248. This corresponds to Book V, Chapter IX, §1 (or V, IX, 1) in Mill's *Principles* on the web-based Library of Economics and Liberty.

government in history – not only in terms of tyranny (jail, torture, etc.) and corruption, but also in providing legalist support for sexism, slavery and ignorance. With "On Liberty" contemplating limits to social coercion over private citizens and "Utilitarianism" and "Subjugation" lamenting laxity in preventing harm to large segments of the citizenry, the brilliant Mill wrestled with issues of property rights and redistribution that so often complicate the realm of liberty and laissez-faire.

Mill's positions had roots in his association with Bentham, whose utilitarian view suggested that society should aspire to its greatest happiness, or highest sum of utilities. Arguing from the axiom of diminishing marginal utility, it followed logically that transfers from rich to poor would be socially gainful. Thus Bentham saw a redistribution role for government in the form of progressive taxation and spending programs. Mill modified that approach, favoring the proportional tax, for example, but channeled Bentham in support of universal childhood education and suffrage over complaints from those who favored the status quo by advocating laissez-faire.

Edwin Chadwick, another follower of Bentham, worked to reform the criminal justice system and strengthen indoor plumbing in London, which proved successful in terms of convenience and public health. This matched nicely with Smith's call for infrastructure and public health expenditures, though it carried the tarnish of imposition by government on many homeowners. The net gain stands clear in retrospect, and today we hardly notice when it comes to building codes that force sewer hook-ups, water quality standards, and mandatory smoke detectors. One might speak of gains in health and safety as enhancements to liberty or as the growth of liberty itself.

Bentham and his followers, including Mill, emphasized efforts to increase the social welfare by directing resources to the poor. Not surprisingly, an opposition arose - arguing perverse work incentives, lost output, unjust takings, impositions on liberty, the evils of radical socialism, etc. Further, as some people seemed to get little happiness from money, no matter its amount, while others seemed gleeful no matter the amount, the logic of redistribution could be attacked at its utilitarian foundation, diminishing and commensurable marginal utility.[36] All these various strands of opposition quickly coalesced into an emerging school of economics, neoclassical economics, focused on prices and quantities determined by equilibrium under perfect competition. Neoclassical economics would stand suspicious of redistributions as advocated by Bentham, Mill, Dickens, and Shaw.

---

[36] If redistribution should flow to the highest marginal utility (as from rich to poor under the assumption of diminishing utility from money), the policy quickly becomes contentious. Imagine people arguing that their marginal utility exceeds that of others on grounds of their weight, height, education, sensitivity, health, etc.

CHAPTER 6

Liberty and Laissez-Faire in Neoclassical Economics

Neoclassical economics turned attention from historical trajectories to propositions about free and independent decision-making. The hypothetical "decision maker" in this vision would be a uniquely optimizing character, all-knowing, self-aware, utterly rational - dubbed *homo economicus* ("economic man" as distinct from *homo sapiens*) by Italian economist Vilfredo Pareto. Thus we are to imagine a theoretical mutant guiding "economies" to efficiency in a state of liberty.[37]

Drawing upon stable metaphysical elements (e.g., production functions, utility functions, and hyper rationality) neoclassical economists proceeded to construct a theory of static markets based on supply and demand (price and quantity) with a market for each and every conceivable product. From corn and cars to candy and computer chips, every commodity would have its

---

[37] Axiomatic and otherworldly, neoclassical economics presumes free and unbridled choice by firms and consumers. That said, many neoclassical advocates of laissez-faire have fiddled with *homo economicus*. Friedman, for example, adjusts the image as follows: "The liberal conceives of men as imperfect beings. He regards the problem of social organization to be as much a negative problem of preventing 'bad' people from doing harm as of enabling 'good' people to do good." Friedman, *Capitalism and Freedom*, 12.

price. The markets in which they were traded would be interactive, connected almost mechanically by the system of prices, so a disturbance in one market would propagate to others, ad infinitum. Question: Could all those markets clear at once under plausible assumptions about taste (utility) and technology (production)?

French economist Leon Walras was the first to theorize the existence of a set of prices, one for each market, at which all markets cleared simultaneously. Given the logical possibility of market clearing, issues of practicality and virtue arose.

Walras himself offered a narrative to open the discussion on social feasibility. His story featured an auctioneer at the center of all trade, groping preemptively by trial and error to discover the unique set of prices at which supply equaled demand for all commodities.[38] Having determined the equilibrium prices, given tastes and technology, trade was allowed, not before, thus guaranteeing an ideal outcome at equilibrium. Though it may seem far-fetched, we can imagine that such an auctioneer represented the market system at equilibrium, which was what his theory supported.

An alternative narrative for the purpose, also implausible, was called "perfect competition." This highly idealized social order featured perfect knowledge, generic products, and the assumption that each and every participant is powerless over prices, so-called "price takers." Competition in this sense involves thousands of producers of virtually identical products, all buyers and sellers

---

[38] The iterative grope by a hypothetical auctioneer was called *tanonement*, distinct from history, forcing all producers into the role of price taker. The process would start with the auctioneer announcing a set of prices for all resources and final goods and services. Consumers and firms would then respond with their intentions to purchase and supply, respectively. The auctioneer would then tally the sum of demands and supplies for each commodity and examine the outcome. If an item's demand exceeded supply, its price should rise in the next round; if supply exceeded demand, its price should fall. Then a new set of prices would be announced, etc. Only when a set of prices is found that clears all markets simultaneously does Walras' auctioneer allow action. Market power and manipulation are mitigated by the auctioneer's patience to grope for equilibrium prices.

making voluntary agreements, fully aware of surrounding circumstances, but utterly powerless over the behavior of others (liberty lurks as the freedom to choose in an environment devoid of coercive power). Not surprisingly, this idea of competition became the centerpiece of economic orthodoxy with its implicit linkage of liberty with laissez-faire.[39]

Competitive markets would grope for market clearing prices at which an "allocation" (of resources and final products) is determined. Given assumptions about production and consumption, economists soon proved that the allocation arising in perfect competition would be efficient. That is, from such an allocation it would be impossible to make any person better off without rendering at least another person worse off. Among other things, an efficient outcome displays no waste in production and the consummation of all mutually beneficial trades.[40] Given an initial distribution of property and talents, all resources are put to work at their highest purpose, GDP is maximized, and no mutually gainful trades are left unresolved.

Intermediate microeconomics introduces this intellectual landscape to students these days, starting from initial endowments of talents and resources, tastes, and technology. A spontaneous and perfectly competitive market system is then depicted with its "efficient" outcome of distributed goods and services. Further

---

[39] Competition and laissez-faire obviously differ. Competition arises in the abstract with an absence of coercive power; laissez-faire arises in historical and social context with significant powers in play.

[40] Economists speak of Pareto Efficiency in honor of the famous Italian economist Vilfredo Pareto. What is Pareto Efficiency? It involves "allocations" of inputs and outputs from which no reallocation can be found that makes at least someone better off without leaving anyone else worse off. Notice that such efficiency precludes waste in production (which could be resolved to make a person better off without loss to anyone) and in distribution (all mutually beneficial trades having been accomplished). Thus we include both technical and distributional efficiency under the umbrella of Pareto Efficiency. This highly theoretical vision implies full employment and maximum GDP, building on metaphysical footings as mentioned: utility functions, etc.

assumptions imply that the system will be self-organizing, robust, and resilient to shocks from outside: weather, war, and politics, for example.

The grand intellectual enterprise distills to a famous theorem: if the conditions of pure competition are met, then the market equilibrium will be efficient. This is the heart of neoclassical economics – elegantly rendered via pure logic, every argument enjoying the ring of formal validity. But because efficiency is not unique (there being an infinite host of efficient allocations, each based on an initial distribution of assets), a second theorem states that any efficient allocation can be achieved as a competitive equilibrium by cleverly tampering with the distribution of property.[41] Very Impressive! The difference between the various efficient allocations arises with redistribution, politically challenging even when gains outweigh losses by a thousand-fold.

Thus we come to the central issues: which of the infinite set of efficient outcomes is best (most just, fair, liberating, etc.), and what reallocation of property might lead to that best of outcomes in competition? If the present situation is best, then laissez-faire is justified. If another feasible allocation would be better, per the higher assessments of morality, fairness, justice, compassion, etc., then reallocation would be in order.[42]

We find ourselves again at Mill's dilemma. How and when should we reallocate property to achieve a better outcome? Who

---

[41] These two basic theorems of welfare economics arose in an era of high theory, featuring such notables as Alfred Marshall, Arthur Cecil Pigou, John Hicks, Paul Samuelson, Kenneth Arrow, and Gerard Debreu. The arguments are typically rendered in mathematical formats: calculus, set theory, topography, algebra, etc. It is an elegant rendition for all to see, if not quite comprehend.

[42] Actual reallocations must arise in the political arena. That said, the branches of economics charged with providing tools to assess economic outcomes using higher order concepts like efficiency, justice, fairness, reciprocity, morality, stability, etc., are called Welfare Economics and Social Choice. Some terms of interest: the "compensation test" (Hicks and Kaldor), "negative utilitarianism" (Popper), and the "difference principle" (Rawls). Theological teachings also enjoy standing.

decides what and how to reallocate? These are decidedly political matters, left by Mill for future generations, perhaps less tolerant of traditional injustices. Meanwhile, the neoclassical orientation, cowed by the political confusion of redistribution or reorganization, quietly anoints the prevailing allocation of property.

CHAPTER 7

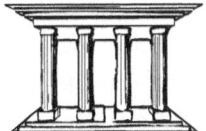

The Planning Debate

M oving from abstraction to worldly affairs, the twentieth century provided distinct historical contexts for discussions
on free markets versus the alternatives of socialism and
economic planning. Following World War I, for example, with an
emergent Soviet Union and its Five Year Plans, Austrian economist Ludwig von Mises advocated the market system against the
alternative of Socialism, especially Soviet-style central planning.
He argued that central planning lacked the versatility and nimble responsiveness of the price mechanism to steer resources to
their most productive uses relative to demand and technological
potential.[43]

A decade later, with economic depression rampant in the West,
Mises attracted an intellectual opponent, Oskar Lange, soon to be
professor of economics at the University of Chicago. Lange imagined that a combination of planning and state enterprises could
do at least as well as the de facto market system.[44]

---

[43] Ludwig Mises, *Socialism: an Economic and Sociological Analysis* (London:
Jonathan Cape, 1936). Published initially in German, 1922.
[44] Lange contributed two papers to the debate: "On the Economic Theory of
Socialism," *Review of Economic Studies* 4 (1936) and "On the Economic Theory
of Socialism, Part Two," *Review of Economic Studies* 4 (1937).

Together Mises and Lange sparked a global debate on the relative merits of two distinct economic systems: decentralized markets versus central planning.[45] Of note, their debate raged in neoclassical abstraction during the Great Depression and steady Soviet economic expansion, and it did not attend to brutal Soviet totalitarianism (early capitalist development in England and America had been fairly brutal too). The debate focused on competing visions of production to fit human needs and wants in the era before computers and big data.

The hotly contested argument came to involve most economists of the 1930s and 40s, virtually everyone agreeing on the pivotal importance of market signals from consumers, ala Smith. At issue was whether managed prices and public enterprises could emulate or even outperform market prices and free enterprise in terms of cost-effective production to serve the consuming public. Mises energetically favored decentralized producers in competitive markets, arguing the inherent efficiency of markets and the impossibility of efficient central planning. Lange favored a plausible planning regime quite distinct from the Soviet system, attending mainly to demands from consumers and producers.

In fact, central planning practiced in the Soviet Union largely overlooked consumer desires, substituting state priorities at Gosplan (the central planning authority). Lange lamented that, suggesting a Walrasian (auctioneer) alternative to inject consumer sovereignty and producer choice into his reformed system. Meanwhile, the Soviet economy moved ahead while depression lingered in the West.

---

[45] This debate had roots in an earlier assertion by Pareto that the competitive market system could be mimicked by a planning regime. Mises wanted to argue otherwise, that no state or planning authority could mimic the market. This was part of a more general thrust against what he called "state-ism." Like most liberals of his day, Mises appreciated that consumers could be wayward, stumbling, and whimsical (differing markedly from *homo economicus*), but he worried more about concentrations of power, including governments, muscular corporations, and central banks. He strongly advocated markets, and saw central banks and legislatures as possible sources of coercion, abuse, and the business cycle.

Following World War II Friedrich Hayek, another Austrian, extended the advocacy of competitive markets. Known for his polemic, *Road to Serfdom*, warning against enslavement (serfdom) via incremental socialism, Hayek focused on the profound vitality of free markets in a world of complex, diffused knowledge and persistently changing tastes and technology. He argued against government intervention in markets on grounds that social planners would be swamped with information, upset with unexpected disturbances, and slowed by bureaucratic processes and delays, still fodder for pro-market sentiments. By contrast, decentralized producers, distributors, and consumers could process vast amounts of information with relative ease via self-correcting markets.[46]

Concerning the debate about planning, John Maynard Keynes praised Hayek's *Road to Serfdom*, but took a stand at variance.

> I should say that what we want is not no planning, or even less planning, indeed I should say we almost certainly want more. But the planning should take place in a community in which as many people as possible, both leaders and followers, wholly share your own moral position. Moderate planning will be safe enough if those carrying it out are rightly oriented in their own minds and hearts to the moral issue.[47]

Planning to Keynes was not intrinsically bad, but widely justifiable so long as it built on proper procedural and moral foundations.

---

[46] Meanwhile, the British and Swedes embarked on their "middle ways," always attentive to the debate raging in economics. Of note, following World War II, the Swedish labor party, having won on a platform that called for more planning, fell back to a more moderate policy system, partly in light of Hayek's *Road to Serfdom*, translated into Swedish during the election.

[47] Roy Harrod, *The Life of John Maynard Keynes* (NY, Augustus Kelley, 1969), 135. The preservation of capitalism was especially important to Keynes who detested Stalin and the Soviet system.

In retrospect, we now see Keynes's insight under a new light, planning techniques having proliferated to virtually every nook and cranny of the modern economy, abetted by computers, servers, electronic payments, and sensors used by powerful marketers and governments. More and more firms employ faster and faster computers and ever more massive data banks to simulate and forecast, to plan, to implement, and to control operations, supply chains, and customers. Who would have thought? Looking back, Keynes may have won the day, as he often did, and his warning stands: "planning will be safe enough if those carrying it out are rightly oriented in their own minds and hearts to the moral issue." The danger today might be that people overlook the historical wisdom that planning can threaten liberty.

While the debate over free markets versus socialist or regulatory alternatives raged in the arena of pure theory, history provided empirical tests of Western free enterprise versus Soviet planning. Especially after WWII decentralized producers of the West performed much better in providing ample supplies of desired food, clothing, appliances, and automobiles. For example, Western European automobiles evolved and innovated to achieve much better performance than their Comecon (communist) counterparts. A well-known point of comparison is the "little stinker," East Germany's Trabant, which did not improve much over thirty-three years, 1957-1990, versus VWs, Mercedes, and Fords that evolved improvements galore. By 1980 a single two-cylinder, two-stroke Trabant produced more pollution than a small fleet of six-cylinder Mercedes Benzes. The free market system was clearly more innovative and productive, which stimulated Gorbachev's reforms of glasnost and perestroika. The relatively weak Soviet performance surely played a part in the demise of the Soviet Union, though that momentous event must be studied carefully lest we come to biased conclusions.[48]

---

[48] See Michael Ellman and Vladimir Kontorovich, Eds, *The Destruction of the Soviet System* (New York: M.E. Sharpe, 1998). The Soviet demise was a

When the new Solidarity government took control in Poland in January 1990 supplies of fresh fruits and vegetables suddenly became available from West Germany, much to the delight of Polish consumers. So too came supplies of used cars, colorful clothing, radios, televisions, spare parts, kitchenware, plumbing fixtures, cosmetics, toys, etc. The Polish people suddenly became availed of higher quality, less expensive goods from the West. Free markets took hold quickly, though many Poles lost jobs and suffered profound austerity in the transition.[49]

Moreover, in its heyday the Soviet system pestered, tortured, and imprisoned people for nonconforming, for religious practices, and for speaking their minds. Millions were sent to the Gulags, and millions more were tormented and tortured in infamous KGB buildings.[50] In spite of official constitutional protections, rights were trampled, adding to the tarnish of perennial shortages and inattention to the wants of consumers.

Interpreting twentieth-century economic events, a parade of inspirational libertarian thinkers has elevated the idea of free enterprise and small government. Robert Nozik's anarchism and Ayn Rand's objectivism fit easily into the pattern, as do contributions by Joseph Schumpeter, Murray Rothbard, Gary Becker, Robert

---

momentous and complex event that requires careful interpretation. Much like homeostasis in ecological systems, social systems tend to have stabilizing features, so change typically comes slowly, often in small steps with periods of calm. The Soviet collapse was sudden. A sign of Soviet era persistence in Russia these days is sometimes called "Ostalgia," longing for the past and desiring to be a major player on the world stage.

[49] For a policy-oriented account of these events, see Jeffrey Sachs, *Poland's Jump to the Market System* (Cambridge: MIT Press, 1993), especially chapter two, "The Balcerowicz Plan", 44-75.

[50] See, for example *Chronicle of the Catholic Church in Lithuania*, now available on the web. This collection of underground pamphlets follows cases of victimized Catholics during Soviet times when Lithuania was a Soviet Socialist Republic. Better known depictions of Soviet oppression appear in literature, especially two books by Aleksander Solzhenitsyn: *The Gulag Archipelago*, (New York: Harper and Row, 1973) and *One Day in Life of Ivan Denisovich* (New York: Bantam Books, 1963).

Lucas, and Thomas Sowell. Thus today's students inherit a deep tradition of optimism, slightly hedged, that free consumers and producers, working independently, coordinated by markets, and with minimal interference from government, constitute the best social organization for matching economic prosperity with political freedom and liberty.[51] That optimistic connection resonates through many titles: *Interventionism* by Mises, *Road to Serfdom* and *Constitution of Liberty* by Hayek, *Capitalism and Freedom* by Friedman, and *The Virtue of Selfishness* by Rand. These powerful teachers deliver a pro-market, laissez-faire message in such plain and straightforward terms that one might wonder why markets haven't been allowed to operate unfettered on behalf of citizen consumers around the globe. Rallying in what some have called "The Age of Milton Friedman," hasn't laissez-faire won in both philosophical and historical terms?[52]

---

[51] Asserting that markets are the best way to organize economic activity has been called a "rebuttable presumption," holding the door against intervention unless or until market performance disappoints. Charles Shultz adopted this approach in his Godkin Lectures of 1976, published as *The Public Use of Private Interest* (Washington DC: Brookings, 1977). There he notes, "A theory of intervention is thus concerned with defining the conditions under which that presumption is indeed rebuttable. We think of the public sector as intervening in private sector, and not vice versa,"13.

[52] "The Age of Milton Friedman" denotes Friedman's influence on the likes of Ronald Reagan, Margaret Thatcher, and their many counterparts. A recent article by Harvard Professor Andrei Shleifer testifies by its title, "The Age of Milton Friedman," *Journal of Economic Literature* 47 (March 2009).

CHAPTER 8

Critiques of Laissez-Faire

"Time after time, the images must be broken, the
iconoclasts must have their way. For the iconoclast
is the soul of man which rebels against having an
image that can no longer be believed in, elevated
above the heads of man as a thing that demands
to be worshiped."   – Martin Buber, theologian

Constitutional authorities around the globe, empowered by
election and concerned for liberty and prosperity, have regu-
lated, restrained, and outlawed a range of activities, including
market activities – crimping laissez-faire. What could those legislatures, administrations, and judges be thinking?

In fact, they have seen situations for themselves and come to
appreciate that laissez-faire amounts to complacency in a world
saturated with injustice, power, and coercion. In Enlightenment
fashion, many political leaders have observed a world corrupted
by monopolists, extortionists, pushers, and predators, a world that
falls well short of optimistic portraits.

Critiques of laissez-faire have come through the pens of venerable skeptics: Malthus, Marx, Veblen, Pigou, and Keynes, to name
a few. Some have seen laissez-faire optimism as otherworldly,

idealized beyond practical sense; some have seen it as ideological, deluded, or incomplete; and some have seen it as opportune support for unbridled power.

Before Adam Smith's *Wealth of Nations*, Bernard Mandeville's *Fable of the Bees* satirized European moralism by depicting prosperity based upon selfishness and greed. Mandeville presented an allegorical "hive" that performed at its best with vices in the driver's seat.

> The Root of evil Avarice,
> That damn'd ill-natur'd baneful Vice,
> Was Slave to Prodigality,
> That Noble Sin; whilst Luxury
> Employ'd a Million of the Poor,
> And odious Pride a Million more.
> Envy it self, and Vanity
> Were Ministers of Industry.[53]

Smith inherited Mandeville's view of private vice as social virtue, but leveled his aim at mercantilism, not morality. Arguing that a semblance of morality would arise in what he called the "system of natural liberty," Smith affirmed "the invisible hand" by which self-interest unwittingly leads to genuine social gain. While he didn't expect morality to abound under the invisible hand, he argued that the market system would outperform its alternative, mercantilism, owing to greater freedom of occupation, faster innovation, and enhanced competition. Government could improve things even further with spending on infrastructure, public health, defense, etc.

---

[53] Bernard Mandeville, *The Fable of the Bees: Or Private Vices, Publick Benefits*, (New York: Penguin Classics, 1989), 66. This corresponds to lines 177-184 of "The Grumbling Hive," Mandeville's poem from 1714 that depicted prosperity arising from self-interest, vice, and vanity, destined to falter when morality intervened. Mandeville coined the term "invisible hand" in this book, and generally anticipated Smith's work.

Thomas Malthus challenged laissez-faire in his pessimistic *Essay On Population*, mentioned earlier, imagining a host of so-called "positive checks" against overpopulation (war, famine, disease, and the like). As an alternative he advocated what he called "negative checks" – most notably later marriage and sexual abstinence to be encouraged by church and state.[54] His friend Bentham suggested that contraception would be more attractive and effective.[55]

Karl Marx offered yet another vision of laissez-faire that he called capitalism. His portrayal of this dynamic social system was highly simplified, characterized by two classes (earning wages and profits, respectively), commodity production, and rising labor productivity, animated by a dialectic of accumulating and innovating capital.

Marx offered many forecasts for capitalism, of which revolution has been the weakest. His more prescient projections included larger and increasingly powerful firms, rising productivity, advertising, a business cycle, an expanding set of commodities, and widespread confusion and alienation. The mechanism of change according to Marx was investment; hence the name capitalism, an era where capital would accumulate and improve as the vanguard of social development.

Challenging Smith-type orthodoxy, Marx saw consumers as products of the capitalist system, susceptible to advertising, conformity, and confusion, thus open to being shaped as needed for profit and accumulation. Because consumers were in no position

---

[54] The French intellectual, Condorcet, had weighed the population issue before Malthus, concluding that humans would anticipate dire prospects and adjust to avoid catastrophe. See Marquis de Condorcet, *Sketching a Historical Picture of the Progress of the Human Mind, 1795*, especially the Tenth Epoch.

[55] Bentham's suggestion of contraception offended Malthus, an Anglican priest. With population growth increasingly checked by lower fertility rates in today's more cosmopolitan world, the voracious human appetite still threatens exponential growth. The issue remains whether laissez-faire constitutes the best way to address such problems.

to guide the system, Marx relegated "consumer sovereignty" to the realm of ideological delusions.[56]

Following Marx, a decidedly American critique of laissez-faire optimism came from economist Thorstein Veblen, who coined the terms "conspicuous consumption" and "pecuniary competition" in his assessment of consumer sovereignty and free enterprise. His examination of the free market system exposed waste at every turn, not efficiency, as consumers emulated the wasteful behaviors of the so-called "leisure class," trying to display social importance by showy, nonchalant spending. He offered the example of a gold-handled cane as a sign of success by which a gentleman could demonstrate his importance at not having to work (who can work while holding a cane?) but retain the capacity to spend freely, meanwhile parading a subtle show of ferocity, weapon at hand. Such is our "barbaric nature" veiled by a thin layer of civilization. So much for efficiency guided by *homo economicus*, now turned out as a brassy show-off. As the public emulates conspicuous consumption, the nation's resources go to showy and wasteful ends.

Turning to production, Veblen saw business leaders devoted more to financial manipulation than to delivering quality products for customers. The businessman according to Veblen answers the ancient urge to capture wealth immediately, now via financial schemes. Calling this acquisitive disposition pecuniary competition, Veblen distinguished business leaders from engineers, the latter concerned with production while the former cared mostly for money. With active markets for financial securities, the businessman could sell stocks, bonds, and notes to create an economy that looked ever more like a casino, more-or-less rigged (to carry the analogy), than an industrial network to support human gain. Veblen went so far as to accuse businessmen of vandalism. "All

---

[56] Marx also saw orthodox economics as ideology, or as a systematic misunderstanding of the world to rationalize the social order. He doubted the prospect of progressive government, and the liberty associated with markets was to him illusory.

business sagacity reduces itself in the last analysis to judicious use of sabotage."[57]

Veblen died in 1929, but he would certainly feel vindicated by an American economy in 2007 with over $600 trillion in derivative mortgage securities atop a real GDP of $14 trillion! Pecuniary competition seemed all the more plausible.

In fact, Veblen's views on human nature varied little from those of Marx, Mises, or Friedman. Like them, Veblen emphasized that human nature featured animalistic, highly predatory, ego dominated behavior to assure self-preservation and social esteem. He differs from others in the extent to which he saw human behavior as institutional or conforming to patterns adopted in community. In short, people play roles, of which conspicuous consumption became famous. Other roles pertain in religion, parenting, dress, etc., to which people conform. Thus he gives us cleverly named patterns of behavior in an effort to depict the free market economy as a clumsy social enterprise, veiled by a delusional sense of individualist efficiency under banners of freedom.

Literary critiques have accompanied economic thought. Charles Dickens famously depicted the plight of people displaced, impoverished, and imprisoned in nineteenth-century England, and John Steinbeck updated such themes for twentieth-century America. In *Grapes of Wrath*, for example, Steinbeck portrayed the problem of monopoly power with the image of a store clerk gouging Ma Joad. There's Ma with the family's pay, a dollar, at the company store. It was a full day's pay, and as usual she found herself in a seller's market, a matter made worse by the insensitivity

---

[57] Veblen's social commentaries caught America by storm, stimulating the formation of clubs to celebrate his iconoclastic disposition. Who but economists, for example, fail to notice that consumption often leads to disappointment, not happiness, or that work can be a major source of satisfaction. Somehow neoclassical theory overlooked these realities while claiming to have the final word on "efficiency" as an expression of genuine human happiness. Veblen focused on such obvious distortions from reality, basing his work largely on the anthropology of his day.

of the sales clerk – who demonstrates the oppressive power of a single seller.

> "Well," he giggled softly, "yes, it's high, an' at the same time it ain't high. Time you go on in town for a couple poun's of hamburg, it'll cos' you 'bout a gallon gas. So you see it ain't really high here, 'cause you got no gallon a gas." Ma said sternly, "It didn't cos' you no gallon a gas to get it out here."
>
> He laughed delightedly. "You're lookin' at it bass-ackwards," he said. "We ain't a-buyin' it, we're a-sellin' it. If we was buyin' it, why, that'd be different."[58]

Back in academe, many eminent professors (led by Pigou, Sraffa, Robinson, Hicks, and Keynes at Cambridge University) delineated conditions under which real-world markets would fall short in terms of efficiency. This line of scholarship, now referred to as "market failure," has its own jargon: externalities, asymmetric information, natural monopoly, interdependency, oligopoly, illusion, and non-rivalrous goods. Externalities, for example, involve third party costs or benefits that are overlooked in bilateral contracts, thus becoming gains and losses that go unaccounted by the market. If external costs generated by a firm exceed its profits, then shuttering the firm might actually add value to the economy. Surely the best-known externalities today, pollution and global warming, involve momentous costs to health and safety, long and

---

[58] John Steinbeck, *Grapes of Wrath* (New York: Viking, 1939), 480. Also recall the car dealer in Oklahoma's dust bowl. "Watch the woman's face. If the woman likes it we can screw the old man. Start 'em on that Cad'. Then you can work 'em down to that '26 Buick. 'F you start on the Buick, they'll go for a Ford. Roll up your sleeves and get to work. This ain't gonna last forever. Show 'em the Nash while I get the slow leak pumped up on that '25 Dodge."(pp. 79-80) "If I had enough jalopies I'd retire in six months." (81) It was a seller's market in which the weak would be exploited and manipulated.

widely ignored by the market system but now seen as burdens upon a veritable world of bystanders.

Defenders of free markets have often argued that the losses due to market failures are insignificant, that corrections would be too costly or chancy, or that time will eventually cure the problem with innovation and competitive entry. For example, when it came to measuring the costs of inefficiency due to monopoly, Arnold Harberger, University of Chicago, rose to the empirical task in 1954, arguing that the estimated costs of monopoly, barely a tenth of a percent of national income, are not worth the bother of repair.[59]

A delightful contribution to market failure literature arose in a paper "On the Stability of Competition" by mathematician Harold Hotelling, then at Stanford. In this paper Hotelling takes aim at the traditional optimism for competition, imagining a beach that is uniformly used by the beach-going public and served by two concession stands. The best configuration of the stands in terms of profitability and service to the public is obvious and would be implemented by any social planner or cartel (sitting at miles 1 and 3 of the 4-mile beach diagrammed, Figure 7).

Figure 7.

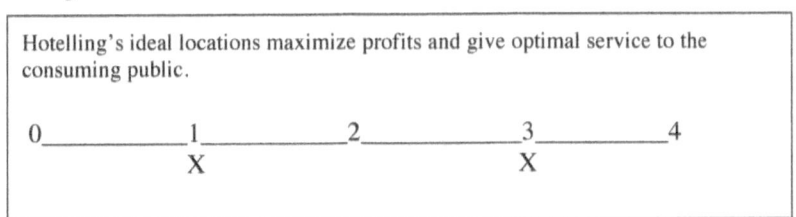

But if the two "firms" were turned loose in unfettered competition, they would migrate predictably, each trying to take

[59] Arnold Harberger, "Monopoly and Resource Allocation," *The American Economic Review* 44 (1954): 84-87. In his conclusion Harberger wrote "When we are interested in the big picture of our manufacturing economy, we need not apologize for treating it as competitive, for in fact it is awfully close to being so."

market-share from the other, until both settled at the center of the beach (mile marker 2) with lower profits and inferior service to the public. The competitive duopoly tends to an inferior outcome that undermines prosperity and confounds efficiency due mainly to interdependence.[60]

While at the London School, Hayek added a methodological critique, expressing distain for attempts by economists to emulate the natural sciences, especially physics. He used the term "scientism" to name the unwarranted overreach of scientific methods into the social sphere. Society was too complex and volatile for standard scientific methods.[61]

Given the many advantages of decentralized markets, some economists have taken up the challenge of momentous market failures by designing corrective patches to the market system that preserve essential market characteristics while enhancing outcomes.[62] This policy approach, called "mechanism design," is best known by the example of "cap and trade" that imposes a cost for loading carbon into the atmosphere. Adding a missing market, so-to-speak, the costs attributed to atmospheric carbon can thus be incorporated into the price system with scarce, marketable permits to pollute. Forcing firms to buy permission to pollute will

---

[60] Neoclassical optimism rests in part on the assumption of independent firms, violated by worldly interdependence whereby a move by one affects others. Hotelling's beach sets up a prisoner's dilemma that challenges optimism for laissez-faire. This line of reasoning has prompted considerable discussion. See, e.g., Albert Hirschman, *Exit, Voice, and Loyalty* (Cambridge: Harvard University Press, 1970), 66-70.

[61] Hayek found support in this view from his friend and colleague at the London School, philosopher of science Karl Popper, yet another Austrian. Not only did Popper support Hayek in his skepticism of "scientism," he went further to argue for what he called "negative utility" in reaction to the neoclassical proposition that happiness and suffering were commensurate under the umbrella of utility. Popper argued instead that the alleviation of suffering ranked distinctly above efforts to increase income for people who are already comfortable.

[62] Leo Hurwicz, Eric Maskin, and Roger Myerson were awarded the Nobel Prize in 2007 for their theoretical work on mechanisms to correct pernicious effects of market activities.

internalize the previously external costs of human-caused global warming.[63]

An unexpected critique of laissez-faire arose from one of its ardent champions, Joseph Schumpeter, yet another Austrian, who updated Marx with a less conspiratorial view of capitalism's dynamic nature. Schumpeter's key player would be the entrepreneur, perpetually disturbing the status quo with new ideas, products, management systems, and technologies. Schumpeter saw natural and entrepreneurial disturbances as primary sources of profit subject to competitive forces of squeeze. Disturbance to him was the essence of laissez-faire, not equilibrium or efficiency. This led to an updated view of capitalism – and to the ironic critique that the system might become too successful!

Rendering market capitalism as a venue for change in history, Schumpeter emphasized a process called creative destruction, whereby new ideas and products displace or antiquate their predecessors. The process would likely come in waves or gales, "gales of creative destruction," as exemplified by the building of railroads in the nineteenth century and subsequently with the automobile and home appliances. The most recent "gale" of innovations has built upon developments in microelectronics including desktop computers, software, Internet, cell phones, laptops, tablets, apps, and more – still reshaping our world of work and leisure in unpredictable ways. Schumpeter's view of laissez-faire emphasizes the episodic destruction of antiquated jobs, products, and ways of life – displaced by new jobs, products, and ways of life.

Schumpeter's focus on change, not equilibrium, suggests that talk of economic efficiency must give way to talk of fitness, resilience, and adaptability. It is the arc of change that must be

---

[63] The global discussion on carbon pricing has focused on carbon taxes, per Nicolas Stern, *The Economics of Climate Change* (Cambridge: Cambridge University Press, 2007). In contrast to setting a high price on carbon to reduce the use of fossil fuels, some economists have argued for subsidies on renewable alternatives. Either way, the goal is to reduce carbon loading with changes in behavior.

noted and assessed in terms of flourishing, stress, adjustment, and extinction. Operating amidst the commotion of capitalism, an ideology built on the logic of equilibrium is at best tangential.

According to Schumpeter change will continue, and even escalate, as long as society can stand the strain. Each gale or epoch would invigorate productivity, stimulate social evolution, and add to social stress. When a society's threshold of tolerance for such tumult is exceeded, Schumpeter imagined a democratic movement toward what he called Socialism. Ironically it would be the successes of laissez-faire and free enterprise that would lead to their muffling, a very modern notion.

> The thesis I shall endeavor to establish is that the actual and prospective performance of the capitalist system is such as to negate the idea of its breaking down under the weight of economic failure, but that its very success undermines the social institutions which protect it and 'inevitably' creates conditions in which it will not be able to live and which strongly point to socialism as heir apparent.[64]

A few paragraphs earlier he had posed the question, "Can Capitalism survive?" His answer: "No. I do not think it can." He was not for socialism, but he could see it coming.

John Maynard Keynes, among the most renowned visionaries of the twentieth century, also saw laissez-faire as an unstable venue, but focused on countervailing its attending business cycle. Sensing recession and depression as endemic blights upon liberty and threats to political stability, he imagined their correctability via enlightened countercyclical fiscal and monetary policies. His ideas proved to be so fertile as to engender "The Age of Keynes,"

---

[64] Joseph Schumpeter, *Capitalism, Socialism, and Democracy* (New York: Harper, 2008), 61.

many elements of which persist in the practice of government leaders, central bankers, and business conditions analysts.

Malthus, Mill, Veblen, Schumpeter, and Keynes were but a few of many heterodox contributors on laissez-faire, liberty, markets, and government. Others included Abba Lerner, John Kenneth Galbraith, Walter Heller, Joan Robinson, and Gunnar Myrdal, who routinely confronted the likes of Mises, Hayek and Friedman. If nothing else, economics features opposing points of view with sparks flying.

Incidentally, an alternative to providing defense, roads, and sewers via government might be to allow an anarchistic market system to do the job. Thus, national defense might be arranged and paid for mainly by the wealthy, as it is their wealth that is disproportionately protected. It's an interesting alternative with free riders galore, reminiscent of Aristotelian magnificence and indigenous Potlatch.[65]

---

[65] See Robert Nozik, *Anarchy, The State, and Utopia* (New York: Basic Books, 1974).

CHAPTER 9

Realities of Power and Influence

Political freedom means the absence of coercion of
a man by his fellow men. The fundamental threat
to freedom is power to coerce, be it in the hands
of a monarch, a dictator, an oligarchy, or a momentary majority. The preservation of freedom
requires the elimination of such concentration of
power to the fullest possible extent and the dis-
persal and distribution of whatever power cannot
be eliminated- a system of checks and balances.
     —Milton Freidman, *Capitalism and Freedom*

The world we inhabit includes powerful players and plenty
of coercion. Facing insensitive power, the less powerful often get their pockets picked, and laissez-faire earns the label
"invisible handshake." But even government intercession can be
ineffective and costly. Such are the complexities of power.

Power itself (the ability to act or influence others in public)
stems from three main sources: money, people, and intimidation.
Thus it can be discerned statistically. For example, The US Bureau
of Economic Statistics estimated that a mere 21,000 of America's
6 million firms in 2007 took in 66 percent of all sales receipts.

Further, a very small group of households controls a disproportionate share of America's wealth and income, the top 1 percent claiming about 36% of the nation's wealth (including houses, land, cars, wardrobes, stocks and bonds). The top 20 percent claim about 85 percent, leaving just 15 percent of the nation's wealth to distribute through 80 percent of its population. Even more extreme, the top .1 percent of wealth holders control as much wealth as the bottom 60 percent of wealth holders.[66] Such are the asymmetries power in relation to money. So begins the avalanche of evidence that economic power is concentrated. As to the other legs of power, people and intimidation, evidence of concentration might be the number of votes in an election or "friends" on Facebook. As to intimidation, one might gather estimates or the number of guns in an arsenal, goons on a payroll, or lawsuits threatened.

We learn a lot about abusive power through common cultural outlets, including news accounts, documentaries, movies, music, books, museums, political contests, and television. Images of power are in the air.[67] A small sample from discography might include Bob Dylan's "Masters of War," Joan Baez's "Prison Trilogy," Woody Guthrie's "This Land is Your Land," and Aretha Franklin's "You Don't Own Me." A sample of poetry might include Langston Hughes' "Let America Be America Again" or Maya Angelou's "I Know Why The Caged Bird Sings;" and literature might offer *To Kill a Mockingbird, Bury My Heart at Wounded Knee, The Godfather,* and even *Travels with Charlie.*

Both political and economic powers are concentrated in the United States. Two parties with two philosophies and plenty of money dominate the political scene, often mired in stalemate. Meanwhile, the economic version of power is more decentralized,

---

[66] The Summer 2013 *Journal of Economic Perspectives* featured articles on income and wealth distribution, including contributions by Mankiw, Alvaredo, et al, and Rosenthal, cited in the bibliography.

[67] The Sociology of Knowledge makes a formal study of how people come to know things, a practical version of epistemology. The study includes modes of transmission and communication.

involving "fellow men" with bargaining advantages (unique products, patents, secret knowledge, golden tongues, persuasive dress, and so on). The situation often features an announced price with a tacit message, "take it or leave it." Most of us routinely face such pricing, and think little of it, perhaps accepting claims that this environment is competitive and efficient.[68] Even when bargaining is allowed it is often to search for the buyer's highest offer subject to satisfactory profit. Thus a door-to-door sales pitch often includes backpedaling, such as "I am authorized to give a $100 discount for an old dictionary. Do you have an old dictionary?" Who has not heard reports of friends sensing a gouge at their banks or pharmacies? Do not be surprised to encounter discriminatory pricing on the web, where a seller there may know who you are and what you like.

Some prices in the system arise amidst considerable competition, especially among sellers at primary sources (growers of coffee, corn, and wheat, for example), but from there prices tend to rise with concentrating power along the supply chain. Prices for many final goods - groceries, phone service, jeans, shoes, and automobiles, for example - are set strategically in offices. With modern advertising and agreements that create or preserve profits, today's prices are increasingly subject to machinations of powerful corporations, interest groups, financiers, and government. The price of sugar in America is supported by federal restrictions on imported sweeteners for the benefit of domestic producers. One is reminded of Adam Smith's lament, mentioned earlier, "In the mercantile system, the interest of the consumer is almost constantly sacrificed to that of the producer." That said, there are signs of competition too, as when a seller willingly matches the advertised price of any other seller.

Though we often hear of America's competitive economy, a public relations drumbeat, there are still relatively few carmakers,

---

[68] The surest sign of monopoly power is high profitability over many decades. True competition would squeeze profits, per Adam Smith.

computer makers, appliance manufacturers, airlines, etc. In their company we find disproportionately muscular banks, brokers, law firms, and financiers ready to facilitate agreements that preempt market forces. Indeed, where innovation and competition arise, expect mergers and acquisitions to preserve power and profit.[69] These maneuvers abet the grip of power, allowing it to persist in conjunction with tools of management science, operations research, budgeting, financial modeling, activity analysis, strategic simulation, etc.

Our "Age of Information" features modern computers, sensors, electronic payments, and software that allow retailers to sense the onset of a pregnancy or a divorce. They can discern in short order that a prospective customer has a cold, or that her mower has broken down, or that he is pondering the purchase of a kayak. Most who browse the web notice pop-up ads soon after. In short, real world capitalism features powerful players exerting influence over their stakeholders (customers, suppliers, shareholders, etc.).

Unions, anti-trust laws, scientific studies, and the free press grew to countervail concentrated and coercive power. Their corrective influence has declined noticeably in recent decades, however, weakened by attacks from powerful employers, price makers, ideologues, and others who claim that such combative elements are counterproductive, even coercive, and that their power should be reduced. Settled science can be denied; the free press can be accused of favoritism; evidence can be overlooked; and power may seem necessary to compete.

Where courts come into play, as they do in criminal cases, anti-trust suits, and political scandals, weaknesses of laissez-faire often come to light. Enron, Anderson Consulting, Merrill Lynch, Countrywide, and Wells Fargo come to mind as examples of corporate corruption. If by chance you are unfamiliar with these

---

[69] During the editing of this essay Microsoft acquired LinkedIn ($28 billion), Abbot Laboratories acquired St. Jude Medial ($25 billion), and Bayer acquired Monsanto ($66 billion), not to mention Sherwin-Williams acquiring Valspar for $11.3 billion. Amid rumors of even bigger deals to come, Qualcomm also bought NXP for $47 billion.

cases, and there are hundreds of them, consider searching for news accounts, court findings, and commentaries.

An interesting example of market power arose in 2015 when Turing Pharmaceuticals acquired the rights to a drug called Daraprim. At the time Daraprim cost about $1 per dose to produce and sold for about $13 per dose, but within a month Turing had raised its price to $750 per dose. Turing's CEO, erstwhile hedge fund manager, rationalized the adjustment, arguing that costs for marketing and distribution had increased dramatically – and that the old price was out of line with market values.[70] More recently we have the case of EpiPen, raising to mind the old saying, "if you find two ants in your living room, you probably have a lot of them." Power doesn't suffer embarrassment.

All things considered, the main worry expressed by people concerned for liberty, including Milton Friedman, is that concentrations of power can lead to coercion. Clearly such concentrated power thrives in our midst, technologically equipped, in both private enterprise and government. As Adam Smith, Milton Friedman and others have noted, government is often complicit in a gouge, as when the US government left American citizens to fend for themselves to fill prescriptions. Many American consumers have chosen to fill prescriptions in Canada where the government negotiates with pharmaceutical companies for more favorable prices on behalf of its citizens.

Surely government can be an effective and efficient supplier, delivering services with exemplary efficiently and fairness: sewage treatment, roads, water, fire protection, playgrounds, and more. Many Europeans enjoy a host of additional public services at relatively low cost, including health care, day care, Internet, and cemeteries. On the other hand, government can be ineffective, costly, coercive and even counterproductive, a subject referred to by economists as "government failure."

---

[70] Back when people saw prices through a moral lens, they would say to opportunistic sellers, "How can you sleep at night charging a price like that?" The expression implied that that a seller should worry about his destination in eternity.

CHAPTER 10

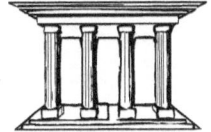

Trends and Trajectories

Informed by widely circulated histories, images, statistics, documentaries, travelogues, and historical reflections, most people have come to appreciate a host of powerful socioeconomic trends: industrialization, urbanization, globalization, concentrated wealth, global warming, and epidemic illnesses. At issue are society's responses to such trends.

The overriding context for this discussion is called The Great Divergence, which shows clearly in charts of income per capita over the past few centuries.[71] Briefly, economic life hovered around subsistence for millennia until sometime in the eighteenth century whence began a profound change. Starting in England and Holland, several nations began to experience economic expansion and rising standards of living. England, Belgium, Holland, Switzerland, and America entered early into this process of expansion, leaving the rest of the world behind. As divergence continued, the favored circle of participants grew while income per capita stagnated elsewhere and even fell in certain regions. The yawning

---

[71] See Kenneth Pomeranz, *The Great Divergence: China, Europe, and the Making of the Modern World Economy* (Princeton: Princeton University Press, 2000) and Gregory Clark, *A Farewell to Alms* (Princeton: Princeton University Press, 2007).

disparity has been closing of late as more regions rise above subsistence with economic development.[72]

What catalyzed and reinforced the historic processes of economic development? This question has animated studies of political economy since Adam Smith.

In the centuries just prior to the divergence most people (over
90%) worked on land and sea in primary activities (agriculture,
forestry, mining, and fishing) with dispersed settlement and relatively stable technologies in agriculture, transport, construction,
and manufacture. A small proportion of people lived and worked
in towns, mainly associated with arts, crafts, trade, administration, and religion. Life and society were very stable, but disturbed
periodically by wars and epidemics of plague and influenza.

Especially during Europe's medieval era, innovations and new
ideas were suppressed as unwelcome or unholy, as if any disturbance would ruin this "best of worlds" under control of kings,
bishops, guilds, and councils. Inventions like shoe jigs, calico cloth,
and woven buttons - when they surfaced - drew heavy fines and
punishments, sometimes including death by hanging or on the
rack. Cloth for Dijon, France, in 1666 should contain 1,408 threads,
including salvages, or so said the Weaver's Guild of that town, and
the town council decreed that nonconforming cloth be destroyed.
At about that time, also in France, tens of thousands were killed
as the authorities tried to contain the illegal flow of calico cloth.
Both possession of calico and its trade were forbidden, death by
hanging among the punishments. Trade was controlled and the
status quo protected; tradition ruled to favor local practices and
products, not to mention social stability.[73]

---

[72] Swedish statistician Hans Rosling has depicted this drama of divergence
and convergence with intriguing displays of relevant data on Gapminder. See
"Gapminder World" at www.gapminder.org, especially "Wealth and Health of
Nations." Also find an entertaining narrative on YouTube.

[73] See Heilbroner, *The Worldly Philosophers*, chapter 2, for elaboration and
commentary. Heilbroner's focus is the emergence of economics as a specialized
study.

The Renaissance and Enlightenment disturbed that social stage, featuring calls for creativity, discovery, and freedom. DaVinci, Galileo, Newton, Locke, Voltaire, Hume, and Kant led a revolution in science and ideas; Columbus, Cook, Magellan, Drake, and others led in exploration and mapping; and on the political front came the emergence of nations, adoption of constitutions, and emancipation of serfs. Somewhere in this social soup came ignition for economic development.

With towns and cities as centers of commerce, pressing for "freedom," an evolutionary process of specialization and trade proceeded within and among nations via agreements and treaties to be administered by courts, governments - and eventually by the WTO's apparatus for dispute resolution. Economic theorists like Adam Smith and David Ricardo provided intellectual impetus for "free trade" in their day, helping in the fight against trade barriers like pirates, robber barons, tariffs, quotas, and licensed monopolies.[74]

By the nineteenth century things had changed: inventions were widely applauded; greed was accepted; and the rambunctious era of capitalism had taken hold. Commercial trade at the fore, innovation had become part of accepted economic jostling.

While neoclassical economists pondered an idealized steady state, the real world of social development featured a swirling universe of change as people confronted predicaments and problems with creative enthusiasm. Distance, disease, exhausted soils, pesky weeds, fires, floods, perishable foods, leaky roofs, mold, hard water, tangled fibers, insecurity, etc., inspired solutions, some of which gave rise to industries: buggy building, bike making, fabric engineering, car manufacturing, food processing, tool and die making, locomotive construction, glass blowing, aircraft fabrication,

---

[74] Smith's call for free trade channeled his optimism about free markets versus the prominence of licensed monopolies in his day; Ricardo's call was more about supporting profit and delaying the Malthusian steady state. Today's barriers to trade arise with fears of corporate power and globalization, manifest in the stalled Doha Round of trade negotiations.

computer manufacture, chip making, software design, cosmetics, chemicals, hybrid seed, GMOs, advertising, etc. More cars called for more filling stations, repair shops, garages, parts inventories, etc., and economic development continued. Not surprisingly, many solutions beget new problems: accidents, explosions, contamination, maintenance, and pollution. New solutions were called for, and the ball kept rolling. Work became increasingly specialized and service-oriented with shrinking employment in primary activities and later in manufacturing. Industrialization would ride laissez-faire as far and as long as it could.

The process of development brought a changing array of jobs as more and more people joined the revolution of contract work. The pattern of employment by sectors has never settled, beginning with 90 percent of jobs in the primary sector (on land and sea) and the rest in manufacturing and services. Over time employment in primary activities fell almost monotonically toward 3 percent in advanced regions, while manufacturing employment rose into the 40 percent range before falling to below 20 percent in advanced economies, the slack taken up by service employments (Figure 8). Service jobs dominate and proliferate in advanced economies, where the trend is for a life of work with many employers, not just one as had been common in the twentieth century. Employment opportunities continued to churn in the cauldron of economic and social development.

Figure 8.

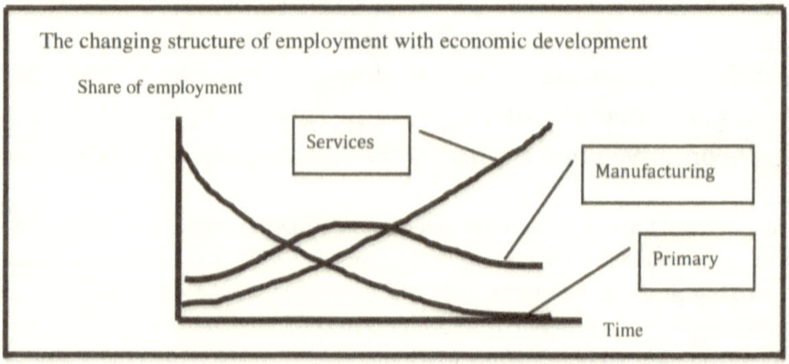

The changing structure of employment with economic development

The market system and its profit motive have encouraged innovation, adaptation, and speculation. Those are perhaps its greatest strengths, giving vent to restless human creativity and problem solving. When copper wire became prohibitively expensive for telecommunications, a substitute for copper was found: nothing; cables now carry signals on laser beams through empty optical fibers. Innovations that stimulate profit get adopted, per Schumpeter, to be squeezed by competition, per Smith, leading to lower costs, massive quantities, and loads of advertising, per Marx.

Few wrinkles of industrial innovation have been foreseen, as exemplified lately by digital computers, developed to compute as the name suggests, but now having morphed into engines of entertainment and control; few computers these days compute in the sense of handling arithmetic. Similarly British railroads came to life as scaled up versions of an amusement park ride; and Speak and Spell, a toy, led to Siri, a conversant search engine. Among the unexpected consequences of development is today's global warming, while extensive "screen time" sometimes leads to neck and finger syndromes, not to mention the restructuring of brain connections, per the discovery of neuroplasticity.[75] And the labor market continues to transform as jobs disappear due to automation. Plowing, spraying, and harvesting can be handled by GPS technology these days, and self-driving vehicles seem to be on the near horizon.

Industrialization and globalization have been attended by massive migration to cities and metropolitan regions. Being commercial centers, cities naturally accommodate trade and serve as incubators for new and expanding businesses. Indeed, cities have many advantages: ready labor, accessible inventories of producer and consumer goods, a growing number of jobs, proximity to specialists in law, accounting, management, and marketing,

---

[75] Neuroplasticity refers to changes in neural pathways in response to demands from society, nature, and the work environment. Finding that the human brain's "wiring" changes with its circumstances suggest that fast-paced social evolution can press biological adaptation.

interesting options for food, fashion, and entertainment, plenty of capital, and global connections. They also house viable markets to be developed and contested. Taken together, cities assemble into a diversified network of volatile trade that is arguably the world's macroeconomic entity.[76] But for setting rules of commerce and distribution, nations are increasingly relegated to political and military entities, bordered and armed, not macroeconomic ones. To an extent even nations are becoming antiquated, the world economy transcending them. What remains is a residue of Welfare States worried about openness, competitiveness, and membership.[77]

In short, the world is increasingly cosmopolitan, a global convergence of settlement and lifestyle featuring unprecedented prosperity. Each city contains active markets and more or less vast streams of capital, jobs, innovative technology, and entrepreneurial energies. So much capital is assembled that the city reaches into the sky and under the ground. Some cities are relatively inert, vested with much less capital and far fewer jobs than their more robust counterparts. It remains something of a mystery why certain cities experience explosive and volatile growth, transforming vast regions, while others limp along and peter out within a few miles of their centers. That said, the global economy features volatile trade and the ascent of new problems, political and economic, including disappointment in the many rural areas from which people are moving, drawn by city jobs and prospects.

---

[76] See Jane Jacobs, *Cities and the Wealth of Nations*, (New York: Random House, 1984) for a lively portrait of economic growth with emphasis on the importance of urban entrepreneurship, markets, jobs, technology, spin-offs, and capital. Jacobs channels Schumpeter's vision of development with a laissez-faire disposition and urban focus.

[77] In the context of a global and cosmopolitan economy the nationalistic enterprise becomes a Welfare State, concerned mainly with the well being of its citizens. Welfare States have always been nationalistic, a fact long appreciated by Scandinavians. In general, a Welfare State faces three key issues: its degree of openness to international competition, its need to stay competitive in key export sectors, and its conditions of membership.

Narrowly specialized rural areas are challenged to compete with highly diversified urban regions that offer niches of work and entertainment for a wide range of talents and interests. That said, small towns have advantages associated with small scale and social connections.

Global urban growth has accelerated, the number of cities with over a million inhabitants having risen from 15 in 1950 to over 350 in 2015. New York was the world's most populous city in 1950 with 12.3 million inhabitants, but fell to 10th in rank by 2015 with 18.6 million, less than half of Tokyo's population, roughly 38 million. In 2016 over half of the world's population was classified as urban, a proportion destined to rise.

Today's bustling, dynamic, and networked city can carry many millions of residents into mainstream prosperity, incubating businesses, ideas, jobs, and capital as it provides ready markets and incentives for competitive entry and further diversification. Its economic energy spreads quickly into hinterlands, pulling young talent away. Ever more tumultuous episodes of development spread through commerce into the global network with disturbances propagating disturbances. Such is the current state of economic development, elbows flying, robots, drones, and artificial intelligence now taking hold. Restless human creativity and economic improvisation have moved forward much as depicted by Schumpeter's process of creative destruction.[78] Today's widespread level of material comfort would rouse the envy of kings only a century ago.

Development has been shaped to some extent by public policy, which can prepare the way with research and infrastructure. But policymakers inevitably play catch-up when it comes to adverse

---

[78] Schumpeter depicted the march of economic progress with terms like "gales of creative destruction" and "swarms of imitators." He recognized that these forces of progress could ebb and flow, even wander over nations like weather patterns. That to him was capitalism with all its tumult and productivity. He favored laissez-faire, appreciating that each episode of economic success would lead to stress and socio-political backlash.

outcomes of health and safety. Such outcomes have been notoriously unpredictable, uneven, and hard to verify. It took decades to confirm that smoking posed a public health threat.

As an outstanding example, America has boomed relative to most other nations in terms of GDP per capita, but she has also displayed high and rising costs for police, courts, health care, and prisons – all of which raise GDP but also raise questions about genuine gain and liberty. Americans today also present significant problems of obesity, stress, depression, violence, drug use, and confusion. According to Surgeon General Vivek Murthy, drug overdoses claimed the lives of five hundred thousand Americans from 2000 to 2016.

Health trends in America are a growing worry with many epidemic conditions riding on social vectors of lifestyle. By comparison, northern Europeans live longer, stay more active, and require less heath care. What's going on? This is a subject of current research, and to some extent it is a matter of consumer choices. Television and sugar are often implicated, referencing stereotypic American inactivity, dietary patterns, and advertising. Sensing the trends in data, the study of social epidemiology seeks to better understand the issue of divergent health outcomes among states and nations.[79]

Concentrating wealth and power are often mentioned as a trend, lately called "the declining middle class." This distributional trajectory has been studied empirically, the middle class having enjoyed a rising share of income – from about 10% to over 20% - between 1930 and 1960, when it seemed to stabilize, and then began falling sometime in the 1970s, more precipitously after 1980. This episode of rise and fall has attracted the attention of economists, research groups, social psychologists, and politicians. Thomas Piketty (2014) elaborated on the recovered share

---

[79] One wonders at the pathways for diverse health outcomes. One hypothesis is that health care has always relied heavily on the internal healing powers of patients. Perhaps those powers are now being compromised with epidemic obesity, diabetes, confusion, and depression in America.

of the top 1% and its likely persistence in his book *Capital in the Twenty-first Century*; Jonathan Haidt (2012) explored its connection to political polarization and social psychology in his book *The Righteous Mind*; and all candidates in the presidential campaign of 2016 tried to address it. Trump's victory rode on his promise to revitalize middle class incomes, or as he put it, "to make America great again."

Lately we have the unexpected but related finding that life expectancy of middle class white male Americans fell over the opening decade of the twenty-first century.[80] In fact, life expectancy for newborns in America, both male and female, fell in 2015.[81] We also have research findings among states and provinces that health at all income levels improves when the least well off gain access to health insurance.[82] What is more, America now finds itself with epidemic depression and violence, increasingly seen as matters of public health. Searching for disease vectors and pathways, a leading hypothesis suggests that ill health seems to accompany lifestyle patterns that correlate with isolation and stress.[83] Perhaps America's individualistic socio-economic system invites burdensome stress relative to societies with greater senses of belonging and membership.

---

[80] Betsy McKay, "Life Expectancy for White Americans Declines," *Wall Street Journal,* April 20, 2016.

[81] Lenny Bernstein, "U.S. life expectancy declines for the first time since 1993," *Washington Post,* December 8, 2016.

[82] To investigate the topic of social epidemiology, especially concerning poverty and health disparities, best to start with facts. See https://www.cdc.gov/minorityhealth/chdir/2011/factsheet.pdf, a four-page pamphlet from the Centers for Disease Control.

[83] See, for example, Daniels, et al, *Is Inequality Bad for Our Health?* (Boston: Beacon Press, 2000), introducing health gradient studies from Harvard University and the University of British Columbia. The emerging field of social epidemiology suggests social vectors of illness as opposed to biological vectors. An interesting variant is the idea that a person's health relates strongly to community. See Pekka Puska, "Successful prevention of non-communicable diseases: 25 year experiences with North Karelia Project in Finland," *Public Health Medicine* 4 (2002).

Studies by Amartya Sen and Martha Nussbaum recognize the imperative of progress, but note lamentable losses along the way. Postwar economic progress impacted adversely in less developed regions around the world, especially when technological disturbances resulted in the loss of what Sen and Nussbaum call "capabilities" that supported and nurtured a good quality of life in long-enduring cultures.[84] In many places the disturbance of labor saving technology left whole communities of people jobless, hungry, and often wandering. This is not new to economic progress; recall the enclosures from seventeenth and eighteenth century Britain. Such plights in developing nations during the 1950s and 60s stood in stark contrast to the United States where the rise in agricultural productivity was compensated by millions of accessible new jobs in metropolitan areas. Less developed nations had no such cushion to fall back upon, and we might notice the similarity with ongoing automation in contemporary America.

Another problematic trend is global warming. What good are property rights, to take a page from the Index of Economic Freedom, when rising seas overtake one's property? How much is liberty crimped when one is confined to quarters by unbearable heat outdoors?

Finally, anticipating future innovations that might threaten liberty, Stephen Hawking and others have warned of a Promethean prospect whereby Artificial Intelligence (AI) might advance to the point of self-awareness and self-interest, leading to the subjugation of humans. Such a prospect, born of trending technology, begs for attention in contemporary discussions of liberty and laissez-faire.[85]

---

[84] Amartya Sen, *Commodities and Capabilities* (Amsterdam: North-Holland, 1958) and Martha Nussbaum, *Creating Capacities: The Human Development Approach* (Cambridge, Massachusetts: Belknap, 2011).

[85] In January 2014 Hawking and others signed an "Open Letter on Artificial Intelligence," encouraging researchers to be alert for prospective pitfalls in AI development. Their concern recalls the Greek myth of Prometheus, who was said to have created mankind and bestowed his creation with fire. He would eventually fall victim to that creation, to be punished by eternal torment. A related story that warns of technological over reach involved Icarus flying too near

Individuals can do little but accommodate these powerful trajectories of history. Thus attention turns to government. Can collective or coordinated action assist with accommodation? If so, what level of government would serve best: state, local, federal, or global? Or might there be technical solutions yet to appear from creative and decentralized entrepreneurs?

the sun with wings made of wax. Both stories exemplify the Hubris-Nemesis sequence, warning of creative/technological predicaments.

CHAPTER 11

On Market Performance and Problems

As for day-to-day life, few dispute that the market system has performed well at supplying food, clothing, cars, books, magazines, houses, purses, computers, glasses, tax advise, legal services, and so on, delivering abundantly what people have wanted. Properly seeded, free enterprise probably explains the lion's share of economic development in the world, provisioning a moneyed public reliably with shoes, haircuts, paper products, and thousands of other things for pantries, wardrobes, shops, and yards. Many a routine problem can be solved readily and inexpensively with a trip to the store – whether you live in the United States, Germany, or China. Moreover, employment opportunities are more varied than ever, making for an enriched life of work for many. Liberty enhanced!

Six advantages of the market system come quickly to mind: First, free markets match nicely with political freedom and personal choice. Second, the profit motive and competition provide incentives to keep costs down, an aspect of efficiency. Third, investment capital inclines to sectors that generate high profit, presumably to meet bona fide wants. Fourth, human creativity is directed at problems of consequence, raising the likelihood of adding value to available resources. Fifth, the relationship between buyer and seller can be impersonal, reducing the likelihood of racial, ethnic, religious, or gender discrimination. And sixth, markets reward quick adoption of cost-reducing innovations and opportunistic arbitrage to handle related problems of glut or shortage.

Of course, it is hard to distill pure market outcomes in a mixed economy. The pure market system simply doesn't exist; so each of us must conjure a sense for its presence, much as we block extraneous noises to focus on certain sounds in communication. We must inevitably draw conclusions about what we imagine the market system to be, knowing that a key element is the voluntary buy/sell agreement. If willing buyers and willing sellers agree on a transaction, and if the object of agreement appears in a large number of transactions, we imagine a market.

Appreciating that most agreements rouse no concern about mutual gain or liberty, we turn our focus to the subset of transactions that raise significant concerns about prosperity and liberty. Among the problems already mentioned are that free enterprise often results in concentrated power (global corporations, price gouging, purchases of political influence), negative externalities (pollution, global warming and climate change, and health risks), and a shortage of public goods (defense, roads, schooling, and bridges). Other problems include adverse and unintended consequences, heavily skewed income distributions, and favoritism/discrimination.

Looking for other adverse outcomes, we see that private enterprises occasionally deliver streams of perfectly legal but relatively pernicious "goods" – tobacco products, soda pop, non-nutritious snacks, super-sized burgers, addictive games, drugs, etc., supported with influential advertising. Common sense and careful research suggest that such products can undermine public health and safety via tooth decay, osteoporosis, heart disease, diabetes, debt, desensitization, and desperate treatments. An accumulation of such adverse effects is sometimes called "illth" (as opposed to "wealth," the accumulation of "goods"), a useful coinage. Sellers hardly advertise such costs, and only a few policies have attempted to intervene. The "war on drugs" and infomercials on tobacco use are obvious examples.[86]

Aside from delivering questionable products, the profit motive leaves some discouraging gaps in coverage. This is to be expected; the profit motive never promised distribution to all; effective demand always required a sufficient number of buyers with sufficient funds. Thus we find that many rural towns today lack doctors, dentists, hospitals, and pharmacies, not to mention grocery stores. Even many cities have large neighborhoods with poor grocery service. Cicero, Illinois, a city of some 84,000 in the Chicago metro area, has been called a "food desert" for lack of full service grocery stores; and many of its small stores are closing, stifled by competition from fast food joints. In fact, the availability of nutritious food has become problematic over much of the US, especially for elderly, low income, and rural Americans. Whether citizens enjoy a right to such services or subsidized services becomes an issue for policy makers.

Judged through the lens of widely accepted social goals, free enterprise has performed poorly in the areas of environmental protection, habitat preservation, civil rights, and universal education - widely desired but not much attended by the profit motive. The federal government intervened in response to poor and declining air quality with corrective policies such as the Clean Air Act of 1963. Almost a decade later the Clean Water Act of 1972 had to overcome considerable resistance as citizens and politicians moved

---

[86] Of course, laissez-faire enthusiasts have sensible defenses for nasty or adverse market outcomes. One is that buyers and sellers acted in liberty. The related hallmark of commercial law is *caveat emptor* or "buyer beware," presuming that buyers are responsible for their choices.

Another defense is that such adverse consequences were unintended. Sellers and buyers were not being careless or negligent, you might say, but came to be surprised as unsavory effects accumulated slowly but surely into consequential problems. This probably applies to chips, burgers, and fossil fuels.

A third defense for laissez-faire against adverse outcomes is that bureaucratic solutions may cost more than they are worth. And even when a bureaucracy proves effective, it tends to linger beyond its usefulness, diverting resources to assure its own survival. Hence, better to do nothing.

to protect water resources following several fires on Cleveland's lifeless Cuyahoga River. That heavily contaminated river notoriously caught fire in 1952 and 1969 – demonstrating that clean water was of little interest to laissez-faire producers, whose liberty to discharge chemical waste hung in the balance. The demand for clean air and water conflicted with the demand to produce without restriction. Such complexity is the normal state of affairs.

As to discrimination, free enterprise historically raised and enforced barriers to housing, jobs, and lending in conformity with racial and gender oppression in the United States. Realtors sorted and guided; banks redlined; and employers discriminated. Indeed, free enterprise was complicit in both slavery and Jim Crow. The simple reality is that demand channels human want, including desires to oppress or seek retribution, and supply caters to demand.

We know from history that proximate free enterprises strongly resisted national parks, inspection, regulation, Medicare, and environmental and consumer protections. Libraries are full of corroborating stories, including Teddy Roosevelt's declaration of the Grand Canyon as a national monument in 1908 against staunch resistance from mining interests. Just a year earlier he had overseen establishment of the Food and Drug Administration (FDA) against similar resistance from the food and drug industries. He captured high ground in Rough Rider fashion, bullying ahead with three legs of public support. First, patent medicines in those days were notoriously diluted, contaminated, and counterfeit; many were simply alcohol with opium or morphine. Second, vendors provided no labeling of ingredients and faced no restraint against grandiose claims. Third, and not to be underestimated, was a book by Upton Sinclair, *The Jungle*, exposing the plight of workers and the quality of products from the meatpacking industry. Consider Sinclair's portrait of making sausage:

> There would be meat stored in great piles in rooms;
> and the water from leaky roofs would drip over it,
> and thousands of rats would race about on it. It was

too dark in these storage places to see well, but a man could run his hand over piles of meat and sweep off handfuls of the dried dung of rats. These rats were nuisances, and the packers would put poisoned bread out for them, they would die, and then rats, bread, and all would go into the hoppers together.[87]

Within a year of Sinclair's publication came two landmark pieces of legislation: the Meat Inspection Act and the Food and Drug Act.

As to questionable products and services, sometimes outlawed, American free enterprise provides gambling, human trafficking, sex, and slaves. Estimates vary, but on the conservative side gambling is a $100 billion industry (net profit, after taxes), casinos alone accounting for almost 2 million jobs. Sex workers, male and female, number over a million and generate at least $200 billion a year; and America is home to at least 60,000 people subject to slavery, many in the sex trade. Tens of thousands in slavery are victims of "bait and switch" schemes whereby an alluring promise results in a vicious trap. Many enterprises and their business plans are scummy from the start.

The market system clearly exhibits mind-boggling complexity. On the one hand, families find wonderful convenience stocking their wardrobes and pantries with well-made clothes and nutritious food from reliable and unregulated producers. On the other hand, private enterprise offers bogus remedies, dangerous products, scams, and other adversities. Markets at their worst offer a venue for people to coerce, threaten, or demean others – a blight on liberty. For a fee you can find someone to break someone else's leg.

---

[87] Upton Sinclair, *The Jungle* (New York: Doubleday, 1906), 135. *The Jungle* also focused on the plight of labor. "As for the other men, who worked in rank rooms full of steam, and in some of which were open vats near the level of the floor, their peculiar trouble was that they fell into the vats; and when they were fished out, there was never enough left of them to be worth exhibiting – sometimes they would be overlooked for days, til all but the bones of them had gone out to the world as Durham's Pure Leaf Lard." 98-99.

CHAPTER 12

Social Goals

Correctives to a society's institutions, markets and government included, typically require explicit social goals to guide assessment and intervention. When speaking of social values or objectives, the idea of commonwealth brings one face-to-face with central issues of political economy: Is there such a thing as "the social interest?" How can it be clarified? Do laissez-faire outcomes match desired characteristics of performance from the community's view? Do outcomes of the economic system (including government) stand up to high standards of liberty, justice, fairness, health, environmental quality, etc.? Is there sufficient work for resourceful, energetic, competent, and hard-working citizens? Answering these questions involves political processes that are notoriously difficult, but how are we to judge outcomes without agreed objectives?

A venerable expression of the social goals approach to efficiency came from Gunnar Myrdal, who shared the Nobel Prize in Economic Science with Hayek in 1974.

> Value premises should be introduced openly. They should be explicitly stated and not kept hidden as tacit assumptions. ... The value premises should

be formulated as specifically and concretely as possible. They cannot be a priori self-evident or generally valid. They should be chosen, but not arbitrarily, for the choice must meet the criteria of relevance and significance to the society in which we live.[88]

In practice, national goals and objectives are revealed, if vaguely, in the language of constitutions, budget documents, appropriations bills, political speeches, enabling legislation, and elections. Thus in practice we speak of national goals concerning freedoms, defense, environmental quality, GDP growth, employment, productivity, price stability, poverty reduction, health and safety, literacy, crime reduction, fairness, and so forth. Goals at the local level may include excellent schools, attractive curb and gutter, safe playgrounds, etc. Given such goals, hopefully subject to measurement and open discussion, the issue is whether the economic and political systems deliver.

Rhetorical complaints about statements of social purpose, values, and goals often assert that such language constitutes a step toward socialism.[89] As communities are complex and non sentient, and as each member of a community can hold distinct priorities and opinions, the effort to specify "social gain" or "social goals" raises the notion of a "social voice" or "socialism." Whether society has a "voice" makes for interesting conversation, highly metaphysical and unending. Further, the practical quest for consensus is

---

[88] Gunnar Myrdal, *The Political Element in the Development of Economic Theory.* (London: Routledge, 1953), 52.

[89] While "socialism" might be implicit in attempts to clarify the community interest or "social goals," it does not follow that adopting social goals implies socialism. One can espouse social goals (extending liberty in the face of racism or anti-Semitism, for example), but be avowedly anti-socialist, whatever that might mean. Generous support for children in Scandinavia and Social Security in the United States are goal oriented, and have been attached to labels like "social democracy" and "socialism." Such words impose ideological ambiguity to public discourse.

notoriously difficult, perhaps a fool's errand, more so at the state and federal levels than at the local and household levels. Such is the political aspect of life, inevitably joined to another metaphysical notion, the economy.

Pondering our evolving system, issues of assessment arise over whether a trajectory of development yields desirable social outcomes. For example, does a particular trajectory promote human health and flourishing? Gratefulness? Responsibility? Courage? Optimism? Sociability? Or does it kindle less desirable traits: illness, anger, fear, hate?

How can diverse and opposing views be reconciled into a set of consistent priorities to guide assessment and redistribution? Many support voting as a constitutional means, though voting can be fraught. In fact, voting has been subject to considerable study over the years, unearthing a host of difficulties, including the "voters paradox" whereby pair-wise voting leads to intransitive outcomes such as option A beating option B and option B beating C, but then C beating A. Thus choices can cycle: first A, then C, then A again, then B, and so on.

In addition we find a profusion of possible voting rules: "priority voting," "plurality voting," and "majority voting" – each with its difficulties (weighting schemes, spoilers, and coalitions, respectively). [90] The framers chose not to allow direct election of President, opting instead for a College of Electors. Whatever the reasons for that, many then and now see wisdom in an elitist approach to government, referring to the likes of Plato and Burke. To wit, "When the leaders choose to make themselves bidders at

---

[90] Kenneth Arrow's Impossibility Theorem suggests that the process of social decision-making should aspire to certain standards, but many desirable standards cannot always be met simultaneously. It's a theoretical point, highly esoteric, but worth exploring. For a quick and entertaining introduction, see Eric Maskin's "Where do we go from here?" (Arrow Lecture, Columbia University, December 11, 2009). For more determined readers, see Kenneth Arrow, "A Difficulty in the Concept of Social Welfare," *The Journal of Political Economy* 58 (1950).

an auction of popularity, their talents in the construction of the state will be of no service. They will become flatterers instead of legislators; the instruments, not the guides, of the people."[91]

Alert citizens, equipped with data and narratives from government, academe, and interest groups, are empowered to weigh all information and vote based on their findings. Whatever goals are adopted, they should bear on all social institutions, subject to constitutional rights and protections, not just markets and government.

Given that economic and political systems are social inventions, one might wonder at this juncture about whether economics is separable from politics. Can the two be pulled apart? Probably not! Property itself is a political construct. And consider the corporation, a fictional but legal "person" whose life began with a charter conferring the rights to sue and to be sued, a valuable lease on commercial life. Corporate mergers, therefore, involve at least two such commercial/legal entities in a strategic contractual maneuver that creates an increment of power at the expense of certain stakeholders (employees, suppliers, consumers). Though corporate charters don't confer the right to vote, corporations have been considered political "people," as in the case of Citizens United v. Federal Election Commission. Thus it is hard to separate the economic from the political. How many transactions don't involve corporations at least in the background or along the supply chain?

Welfare Economics and Social Choice are the branches of economics charged with providing tools and evidence that can be used to assess social institutions and economic outcomes, making use of higher order concepts like efficiency, fairness, justice, reciprocity, morality, stability, etc. While the notion of efficiency often dominates, being the primary focus of economic orthodoxy, other more philosophical standards are no less important. John

---

[91] Edmund Burke, *Reflections on the Revolution in France* (New York: Holt, Rinehart and Winston, Dover Edition, 2006), 277. Plato preferred elite "philosopher kings" to democracy, expecting democratic decay to tyranny.

Rawls famously asserted that justice is to institutions as truth is to propositions. "A theory however elegant and economical must be rejected or revised if it is untrue; likewise laws and institutions no matter how efficient and well-arranged must be reformed or abolished if they are unjust."[92]

---

[92] John Rawls, *A Theory of Justice* (Cambridge: Harvard University Press, 1971), 3.

CHAPTER 13

Corrective Policy

Markets and other social institutions reside in constitutional environments subject to interventions according to constitutional procedures. Presuming that unfettered markets and free enterprise constitute the best economic foundation, we imagine a government exerting minimal effort to provide conditions for market activity: property rights, rules, and courts to adjudicate disputes. From that start the default disposition is laissez-faire or free trade, watchful for instances where adverse outcomes might justify politically approved intervention by constitutional authorities. Thus we see public policy as corrective intervention, responding to problems in the constitutional system.

When it came to pernicious lead contamination along roadsides, citizens and their representatives saw a problem to which the market did not seem to attend. They sought correctives through the political system, where policy economists suggested an extra tax on leaded gas to undermine its demand in the market (research having suggested that consumers would avoid the tax by switching to unleaded fuel). But legislators were reluctant to raise taxes; they chose instead to implement a regulatory scheme that proved costly and slow to deliver results.[93] Such is the American process: the public demands; economists advise; and constitutional authorities decide.

Of course, no policy is perfect, and some are deeply flawed from the start. Why? For one thing constitutional authorities, especially legislative bodies, contain a disproportionate number of lawyers, which invites a bias for command-and-control regulation over less restrictive, market-type incentives. "Thou shall not ..." is a paradigm of law, so even though regulations notoriously antagonize, expect regulatory correctives. Further, there seems to be a "do no harm" penchant in legislatures that complicates policy formation. Anticipating and compensating losers makes for clumsy legislation and a subsequent clamoring for membership in the class to be compensated.

The policy against acid rain provides a worthy example. Determined to reduce atmospheric emissions of sulfur oxides from coal-burning factories and power stations, Congress decided on a regulatory approach with its Clean Air Act of 1963, though little was accomplished until the Clean Air Amendments of 1970. By then administrative details could be handled by the Environmental

---

[93] In 1970 motor vehicles emitted over 156,000 metric tons (343 million pounds) of toxic lead into the atmosphere, but amidst a growing realization that this lead was poisoning the atmosphere and contaminating roadside soils. As to regulatory disappointments in the battle against leaded gasoline, the biggest was called shirking or "fuel switching", whereby people pumped leaded gas into cars designed for and mandated to use unleaded gas. Switchers simply bored open the inlet restrictor to the fuel tank (allowing the larger leaded gas nozzle) and cut off catalytic converters (which would be fouled by lead). This practice was widespread, with EPA estimates of shirking ranging from a low of twelve percent of cars sampled in Pittsburgh to a high of twenty-six percent in Orlando, Florida. It turned out that a nickel a gallon was incentive enough for many to shirk. Meanwhile the cost of enforcement and adjudication were also high. The gas tax, had it been deployed, would simply have involved an upward calibration of the tax on leaded gas at the pump, where a tax was already levied. It would have incentivized the use of unleaded gas, generating little revenue and quickly modifying behavior. Even people with older vehicles probably would have switched to unleaded gas and poured a cheap lead additive into their tanks.

Protection Agency, established by Presidential Order (Nixon) to set standards for air quality and oversee the requirement that "scrubbers" be installed in the emissions stacks of fossil-fueled power stations. This solution was problematic for several reasons. First, once a scrubber was installed there remained little or no incentive to reduce emissions further; compliance was good enough. Second, expensive scrubbers may not have been the best solution in terms of abatement or cost, but locally appropriate alternatives were not authorized. Third, legislators recognized that low-sulfur coal was expensive and that less costly petroleum products would elbow the coal industry. In 1974, following OPEC, several court cases, and the call for energy independence, new legislation urged the conversion of plants from oil to coal, subject to EPA approval. As might be expected, this gave rise to costly legal maneuvers that in turn led to more regulations, etc. Things got complicated fast, and the regulatory approach grew more unwieldy and rigid.

At the outset, economists had expressed a strong preference for market-type incentives instead of regulations. The favorite option was to levy a burdensome tax on unwelcome emissions and let polluters find ways to abate those emissions in the coincident interests of profit and the environment. That would incentivize polluters to find cost effective solutions at fairly low cost to government. Nicolas Stern famously proposed a similar strategy of "carbon tax" to reduce the use of fossil fuels in the fight against global warming.[94]

Why use coercion of any kind to steer behavior? It is a matter of social goals, noted earlier. Many consumers and producers may not care about the environmental effects of lead contamination, acid rain, or global warming, but society at large mobilizes around a collective sense of being harmed or damaged. The Constitution allows such public priorities to take precedence over free enterprise

---

[94] Nicolas Stern, *The Economics of Climate Change* (Cambridge: Cambridge University Press, 2007).

according to approved procedures of legislation, administration, and review. Economists may advise, but legislatures rule.

That said, regulations work best in certain relatively desperate cases. The infamous story of kepone, for example, involved dangers too extreme and proximate to be tolerated at all, so strict regulation made sense.[95] For another story, British bureaucrats and Parliament overcame household resistance in the eighteenth and nineteenth centuries when they promoted and then required indoor plumbing and sewer hookups in London. The bureaucrats were responding to findings on public health, but faced citizens who resented the expense. Luckily those same citizens appreciated the prospect of less smelly neighborhoods and the convenience of ready water at the tap. Only afterward did they appreciate the dramatic abatement of water borne diseases, including Cholera, Typhoid, intestinal parasites, Giardia, E. coli, and worms. Flush toilets added further to public health.

Public finance is the branch of economics devoted to the study of public revenues and expenses. All branches of government are considered, though levels and proportions of spending vary by state and locale. The largest share of state and local spending overall goes for education and training (about 33 percent); highways and police protection get less (at about 6 and 4 percent, respectively).

The first Nobel Prize in Economic Science was awarded jointly to Ragnar Frisch and Jan Tinbergen for their empirical work on economic relationships. Recognized as pioneers in the field of econometrics, they sought to clarify, among other things, the connections and quantitative sensitivities between various policy instruments and outcomes. Our concern has focused on two

---

[95] Kepone was produced and sold as an insecticide by a company in Virginia. It was famously released into the James River, causing fish kills and endangering both wildlife and humans. The river had to be closed to fishing for over a decade from Richmond to Chesapeake Bay (about 100 miles). The story stands as an infamous case study in environmental policy. In 2011 the Stockholm Convention on Persistent Organic Pollutants banned kepone worldwide.

abstract instruments, free markets and government intervention, and two related goals, liberty and prosperity. This level of abstraction continues to challenge the number crunchers, so we have proceeded in abstract terms with examples.

Citizens and politicians alike want to find clear propositions to guide public policy, abetted by science, but in fact the effects of policy generally depend on context and compliance. Such ambiguity puts things into the realm of relativism or relativity. Einstein provided instances of relativity for cosmology, arguing that gravity affects time; it boggles the mind to think that in the near singularity of a black hole time virtually stops as space expands. A kindred example, less challenging and closer to home, concerns the weight of clouds. Many will say that clouds have no weight, as they float; but that would be a false conclusion. That clouds are lighter than air does not imply that they have no weight. In fact, your average storm cloud weighs on the order of 100 million tons, a fact that becomes apparent when you account for its rainfall.

Though the idea of relativism can spark controversy, especially in the moral realm, most folks will understand that a tax incentive may serve well for certain goals at certain times and places, but not at other times or places. This is important in an era when tax cuts are widely thought to "prime the pump" for a virtuous cycle of employment and income formation. But be advised that America's experience with tax cuts has been uneven.

The 1964 tax cut stimulated GDP as predicted by Keynesian models, reinforcing expectations. But then came the so-called "supply side" tax cuts of 1981, animated by a reading of history called the Laffer Curve, and events did not unfold as touted. In the subsequent seven years of peacetime, 1981 to 1988, the national debt tripled while the US fell from its standing as the world's largest creditor nation to being the world's largest debtor nation. That had not been the idea behind those tax cuts, though most economists had warned of it. Further, when Reagan left office in 1989 incomes were routing from middle-income households to high-income households, returning to a pattern typical through the early decades of the twentieth century when the top 1 percent got between fifteen and 20 percent of national income. That distribution changed after World War II, so between 1940 and 1975 the share going to the top 1 percent sat at about 9 percent while the middle class share went up. Then between 1976 and 2011 the share of income for the top 1 percent returned from 9 percent back to 20 percent while the middle class share fell.[96]

Two decades later the Bush tax cuts of 2001 and 2003, including cash rebates, generated such a disappointing economic stimulation as to inspire the National Academy of Sciences to investigate what had changed in the American economy. Its special commission gave a name to the economic malaise, "Gathering Storm," but its focus was not on taxes so much as on profound slippage in the nation's preparation of engineers and technologists. Unfortunately the Commission Report came at the onset of America's Great Recession and went unnoticed.[97] By then observant economists had realized that the effects of tax policy depended upon the choppy waters of history, and that a new mode of policy was needed. Stuck in its old rut, Congress responded by

---

[96] According to Thomas Piketty, *Capital in the Twenty-First Century*, (Cambridge, Massachusetts: Belknap Press, 2014) and Facundo Alvaredo, et al, "The Top 1% in International and Historical Perspective." *Journal of Economic Perspectives* 27 (2013), the twenty percent share of income taken by the top 1% of late is likely to persist, having rebounded to historical levels following a series of new technologies and cuts in the highest marginal tax rate. The first cut came in 1964, lowering the maximum rate from 91% to 70%, which is where it stood until 1981. By the time Reagan left office in 1989 the highest marginal rate had fallen to 28%. In 2016, the highest marginal rate is 39.6%, applied to taxable income above $400,000. Other reasons for the rise of the top 1% focus on the control of receipts from advanced technology.

[97] The 2007 report, *Rising Above the Gathering Storm: Energizing and Employing America for a Brighter Economic Future* (Washington, DC: The National Academies Press, 2007), offered many recommendations focused on the development of the nation's human resources. The report was prepared by the Committee on Prospering in the Global Economy of the 21st Century, headed by a blue-ribbon team from industry and academe. The report remains available for purchase or browsing on the Internet.

pointing fingers all around – one side calling for tax cuts and the other for increases.

Things get even more complicated when correcting for damages borne by third parties whose interests have been excluded in market transactions. Various stories of pollution exemplify the plight of innocent victims in free markets. The infamous Donora Smog of 1948, for example, a byproduct of local steel manufacturing outside Pittsburgh, killed at least twelve prior to the Clean Air Acts.[98] Such damages could be adjudicated in the aftermath through courts or perhaps prevented by corrective policy. At the base of both court cases and preemptive policy are damages caused by "neighbors" claiming to be independent individuals with rights to engage in free enterprise. Clearly discernable damages can trigger Mill's "harm to others" condition for coercive intervention.

Turning from production to consumption, what should be done when consumers buy things that add momentarily to happiness but vandalize public health? Tobacco comes immediately to mind. Today's fast foods, sodas, e-cigarettes, and sundry excitements seem to have led to epidemics of obesity, diabetes, confusion, drug use, and gun violence that inspire widespread concern but little yet in the way of policy. Many observers pin their hopes on education, but others argue for a more heavy-handed approach. Meanwhile, public attitudes and political machinery churn, looking for answers. It took decades to ban smoking from public venues, and that was relatively easy.

As to policy intervention, an extreme regulatory tool is to ban products. This form of intervention generally arises in the interest of health and safety, in keeping with police powers. But the debacle of Prohibition still haunts, toying with moralistic paternalism and costly enforcement.[99]

---

[98] For more on the Donora smog, see Devra Davis, *When Smoke Ran Like Water, Tales of Environmental Deception and the Battle Against Pollution* (New York, Basic Books, 2002) or search for Donora smog.

[99] Not all paternalism is bad or unwelcome. Medical care tends to be paternalist, as do many innovations in respectful theories of choice. See the literature on

Banning dangerous or pernicious products carries a negative tone for at least two reasons. One concerns liberty, as consumers vary: a glass of beer might be a gain for one person, a benign indulgence for another, and a slip to devastation for yet another. Each consumer must discover for herself whether a product is gainful, and then muster the discipline to behave responsibly. Liberty allows for varied lifestyles, discipline not required. The second pertains to market mechanics, as black markets inevitably emerge when products are controlled or banned. Prohibition and the War on Drugs clearly indicate that banned commodities flow in black markets alongside illicit bets, slaves, and hit contracts with the consequence of turning consumers into criminals. In time the costs of enforcement often escalate and the specter of government failure looms.

Fraud and secrecy can pose problems for market activity too, but it is difficult to prove criminal intent in the context of *caveat emptor*. Tobacco companies have been sued successfully, as have car manufacturers, for hiding known risks from consumers. These cases took decades to adjudicate at great expense and with the complication of countervailing scientific studies.

Concerning rigid social institutions and traditions like oppressive racism and sexism, correctives have come via Executive Order (Lincoln's Emancipation Proclamation and Truman's Integration Order), court rulings (Brown v Board of Education and Loving v Virginia), and legislation (Civil Rights, Voting Rights, and Equal Credit Opportunity Acts). When it came to integrating schools in Arkansas, federal troops and state militias were deployed to impose new rules on a resistant public that favored the discriminatory status quo.[100] Liberty grew for the oppressed, and the freedom

---

"libertarian paternalism" and the architecture of choice, including strategies of "opting in" versus "opting out." A classic in the field is Richard Thaler and Cass Sunstein, "Libertarian Paternalism is Not an Oxymoron," *University of Chicago Law Review* 70, (2003).

[100] President Eisenhower deployed troops to Little Rock, Arkansas, to assist with the racial integration of public schools. Though racial hatred and tension have

to discriminate was bounded for their oppressors, but such gains excite social strife and insurgency. Such resistance shows clearly in the cases of racial and gender discrimination, but it is the norm for most interventions: road construction, environmental protection, reproductive rights, etc.

So it goes as we interpret policy intervention from the view of liberty and laissez-faire. All policy decisions are political, policy design and implementation being multi-disciplinary, multi-specialty enterprises.

---

abated, they remain significant; witness Black Lives Matter and the term "white fragility" in this twenty-first century.

CHAPTER 14

Reform and Repeal

We trained hard, but it seemed that every time we were beginning to form up into teams, we would be reorganized. I was to learn later in life that we tend to meet any new situation by reorganizing; and a wonderful method it can be for creating the illusion of progress while producing confusion, inefficiency, and demoralization.

> \- Attributed, but falsely, to Gaius
> Petronius Arbiter, Roman, BCE

Once instituted, a policy assumes a life of its own, evolving in the complexity of administration, legislative review, courts, and markets – not to mention weather, war, political maneuvering, and the business cycle. As with all enterprises, a public policy must persevere with disenchanted employees, disrupted supplies, disgruntled customers, legal complications, confusion, and thousands upon thousands of details.

Being imperfect, policies are always subject to reform and the possibility of repeal. A program that made good sense in 1950 might have become outmoded or even counterproductive by 2000.

Or it may have got off on the wrong foot from the start and evolved in a clumsy way to a state of dysfunction or escalating cost.

For citizens who want to be involved, "fishbowl" government provides plenty of information via easily accessible budgets and reports.[101] Budgets anticipate and rationalize the spectrum of public spending up to a year ahead; appropriations allocate funds by program to be spent in the current fiscal year; annual reports look back over the prior year at how money was actually spent; and various analyses speak to net benefits in terms of goals and costs.

Very few citizens get involved or consult public documents, leaving representatives to watch for problems and possible improvements. But as every reformer learns, it is exceedingly difficult to influence or repeal a policy.

Reforms are often the hallmark of an era. The Nixon Administration proposed a Negative Income Tax as welfare reform (ala Friedman) and a relatively enlightened single-payer National Health Care Program, but neither moved through Congress. His presidency is known instead for strengthening environmental protections, opening the door to US-China relations, and Watergate. The Carter Administration famously deregulated the transportation industry (the Airline Deregulation Act, the Staggers Rail Act, and the Motor Carrier Act). The Reagan administration became known for its energetic efforts to cut taxes, reform New Deal programs, and weaken environmental protection. Jumping to the Clinton administration, two reforms stand out: welfare reform and financial services reform. Of course, none of those reforms was perfect, but each gained approval. The financial sector reforms of 1999 have proven especially controversial.

To elaborate on the process of policy evolution, consider the

---

[101] For the federal budget proposal, FY 2017, see https://www.whitehouse.gov/omb/budget/Overview or search for "US Budget." Citizens rarely apprise themselves of public documents or other information sources, and studies show that voters are poorly informed about the details of their government. For information about state and local government finances, visit the Urban Institute at http://www.urban.org/.

policy that came to be called "Welfare." It began in 1935 as an element of Social Security designed to help single mothers – mainly white mothers - stay at home with their children. Called Aid to Dependent Children (ADC), it provided a modest $18 per month for one child and an additional $12 per month for a second child. Over decades the program offered light support to children, including many whose fathers were killed in World War II, but it provided only small payments until Johnson's War on Poverty raised the ante and renamed the program Aid to Families with Dependent Children, AFDC. When subsequent research suggested that AFDC had the unwelcome effects of welfare dependency and family destruction, especially in the African American community, reformers suggested replacing it with a Negative Income Tax, as proposed by both Nixon and Carter. Both proposals failed, eventually leading to "Welfare Reform" in 1996 when President Clinton signed into law the Personal Responsibility and Work Opportunity Act. That reform has had its unintended consequences too, including increased incarceration and higher rates of poverty. Stay tuned. Guaranteed income programs still seem possible, though Swiss voters rejected a guaranteed income proposal as welfare reform in 2016.

For a longer-term example of policy evolution and reform, consider public education – still a bright frontier for liberty and widespread prosperity. The word "education" does not appear in the United States Constitution, but arises as a responsibility of government in every state constitution. Thus each and every child in America enjoys a constitutional entitlement to a certain amount of schooling. To comply, every state divides itself exhaustively into school districts, each with an elected board that is responsible to administer requirements and available funds.

As some districts have more resources than others, every state has adopted a so-called "funding formula" to balance resources among school districts by means of variances and grants. The word "formula" refers to an accumulation of laws, procedures, and court findings, so no one knows exactly what it is; related disputes are handled via district administrations and state courts. Still, some districts devote more resources to students than others, which raises the specter of discrimination in the entitlement. Several state courts have decreed that all districts in a state should deploy a common level of funding per pupil. For example, in the case of Serrano v Priest the California Supreme Court mandated that education funding be divided equally on behalf of students, giving rise to state control of funding for all public schools – though subsequent adjustments have weakened the policy for equity in funding public education. Many other state Supreme Courts and legislatures have decided and acted similarly.

Out of frustration with formulas, curriculum, and other aspects of public schools, many families have chosen to send their children to private schools or to provide schooling at home, after which they have become less inclined to support referenda in support of public schools.[102] And so it goes, with periodic spates of reform at the district and state levels. Such is the nature of our highly fragmented constitutional system.

Among perennial suggestions for reform is the call for decentralization, moving against the trend of growing federalism. Nixon advisor Edward Banfield wondered thoughtfully at the federal government's willingness to fund road expansions for reduced congestion. He saw such road expansion as catering to local "comfort, convenience, amenity, and business advantage," which to him did not rise to the level of federal aid – especially given effective, low cost alternatives available at the local level: car pooling, staggered work schedules, rapid transit, and various schemes of "electronic

---

[102] Frustrations with public schools have risen on many fronts, not just funding formulas. Many families have pulled their children from public school for curricular reasons (teaching evolution and reproduction as science, embarrassing narratives as American history, or sacred texts as literature), because of teachers and teacher unions, and resistance to busing for racial and ethnic integration. For an interesting account on state requirements to teach Creationism as science, see Langdon Gilkey, *Creationism on Trial*, (Charlottesville: University Press of Virginia Press, 1985).

road pricing." He lamented the lack of political will at the local level – where politicians and citizens preferred to have others pay for their preferred road improvements. [103]

But for protecting civil rights and constitutional freedoms, sometimes less likely to arouse local concern, decentralization enjoys considerable support from politicians and economists focused on efficiency. If public services could vary in scope and quality at the local level, then people could avail themselves of a preferred mix of government services by "voting with their feet." Some citizens would want fancy curb and gutter, to give an example, while others don't care about that; and similarly with parks, playgrounds, green spaces, schools, trash collection, road maintenance, and sidewalks. Households could locate accordingly, neighborhood by neighborhood.[104]

Of course, nations, states, and cities differ in their capacities to reform. Some are relatively nimble due to greater homogeneity, smaller scale, more trusted leadership, or a tradition of dispute resolution and cooperation. Many nations have updated their constitutions over the past fifty years (expressly advocated by Jefferson on grounds that a generation should not be allowed to bind successor generations). Sweden's constitution dates from 1974, for example. By contrast, the United States Constitution dates from 1778, and while a major revision would seem politically impossible, many significant reforms have been suggested: division of states making for a larger number, regional currencies, more explicit protections for women against crimes of unwelcome advance and rape, majority voting for President, limits to campaign funding,

---

[103] Edward Banfield, *The Unheavenly City Revisited* (Prospect Heights, Illinois: Waveland Press, 1975), 4-7.

[104] The idea of decentralizing government arises clearly in Banfield, *Unheavenly City* and Charles Tiebout, "A Pure Theory of Public Expenditures," *Journal of Political Economy* 64 (1956). Their suggestions have proven problematic on many fronts, mainly due to the promotion of social sorting leading to local uniformity of traits and outlook, including the potential for ghettoes and ethnocentric tribalism.

more setting aside of land as conservation reserves, and an explicit national responsibility to protect water resources. As it stands, these changes can be achieved one-at-a-time by constitutional amendment, also a difficult process.

Policies need not be uniform across time or geography. In the 1950s and 60s Sweden pursued a policy of promoting migration from weak areas to thriving cities, following the vision of Gosta Rehn, while Erik Brofoss led Norway in the opposite direction with a policy to resist migration by promoting job growth in economically weak areas of the nation. Though these policies differed in the extreme, each made sense in its national context.[105]

China moved from a disappointing era of State Capitalism under Mao into an era of expanding Venture Capitalism following courageous prompts from Deng Xiaoping. No doubt the Chinese system will continue to adapt. Its One Nation Two Systems approach from 1997 has already moved to the urban centered development model of the West, but with an elitist central government that faces demands from citizens for more authority. What an interesting place to study liberty and laissez-faire!

Many point to Milton Friedman as a role model for policy reform. Keenly observant, informed, tenacious, and widely respected as a spokesperson of the Chicago School, he deserves special attention. His books, lectures, and interviews continue to enjoy a global following, espousing a practical suspicion of government intervention to the point of tolerating a host of laissez-faire problems, including monopoly power. Expressing supreme confidence in free enterprise, Friedman railed against "government failures" in the areas of farm support, social security, fixed exchange rates, discretionary central banking, licensure, and more.[106] He was a

---

[105] Steven Soderlind, "Particularly Polar Programs: Social Economics and Divergent Settlement Policies in Postwar Scandinavia," *Review of Social Economy* 70 (2012) introduces the seemingly contradictory policies of Sweden and Norway following World War II.

[106] See Friedman, *Capitalism and Freedom*, 35-36, for a list of fourteen programs that he targeted for reform.

dogged fighter for reform and repeal whose voice somehow rose above the cacophony of professional economists.

As to critical perspective, be alert for Friedman's infectious optimism, sometimes toying with the tenuous connection between ideal competitive markets and laissez-faire. The two are very different, historically and intellectually. Competitive markets are idealistic, presuming rationality, intense arbitrage, and the weak position of "price taker" for all buyers and sellers. In contrast, laissez-faire implies a free wheeling milieu, complex and worldly, power and maneuvering in play, where deals are made to preclude market forces. Laissez-faire cannot claim "price taking" or "efficiency," let alone freedom from abusive power or unwarranted discrimination. That said, Freidman's wisdom is to warn of adverse effects from government intervention, especially on the regulatory side, in light of ideal, somewhat conceivable market activities.

None of this is to say that government should be small or large, active or inactive. That is a matter for the constitutional system to work out. Nations and states will differ. The point is that persistent adaptation and rebalancing of public policies must be a theme of government everywhere. People who see government as a static element on the stage of history are as heretical as those who see the economy in static terms. Neither makes practical sense. Better to presume that there is no perfection; the inevitable processes of change are always in play. Again, we find ourselves on the soapbox of social relativism; the best policy for this place or this time may not be best for another place or another time.

CHAPTER 15

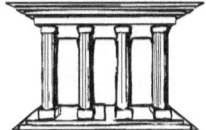

Mill on Justice, Taxation, and Inheritance

Having assumed leadership over economic orthodoxy and libertarian sentiment in nineteenth-century Britain, John Stuart Mill deserves special attention in discussions of liberty and laissez-faire. Many of his publications are germane: *On Liberty, Utilitarianism, On the Subjugation of Women,* and "Of the Grounds and Limits of the Laissez-faire or Non-interference Principle." All told, he left a high-water mark on matters of concern here.

Working from the dismal science,[107] Mill saw economic output (GDP) determined primarily by available resources and largely independent of its distribution (the degree of independence being an empirical matter, not knowable *a priori*). Characterizing economic growth as "increased command over the powers of nature," he correlated distribution with justice, not efficiency, and he discerned that distribution arose according to social conventions that could be examined and revised. Thus he poked at his readers:

---

[107] The "dismal science" predicted an eventual steady state of economic output to be distributed over three classes as rents, profits, and wages. Building on Malthusian assumptions and fixed technology, the dismal view was that steady state wages would cover bare subsistence and profits would approach zero, thus leaving a large windfall of rents for the landed class that would capture much of a nation's wealth without having done much for it.

> Even what a person has produced by his individual
> toil, unaided by any one, he cannot keep, unless
> by the permission of society. ... The distribution
> of wealth, therefore, depends on the laws and cus-
> toms of society. ... Society can subject the distri-
> bution of wealth to whatever rules it thinks best:
> but what practical results will flow from the oper-
> ation of those rules must be discovered, like any
> other physical or mental truths, by observation
> and reasoning.[108]

Liberty was to Mill a high priority. "After the means of subsistence are assured, the next in strength of the personal wants of
human beings is liberty."[109] Thus he pondered future government
programs that might enhance both liberty and justice, programs
that lay beyond political reach in his day.

For the sake of justice he envisioned a system of distribution wherein everyone earned their incomes by productive effort
and everyone paid the same fixed proportion of their income in
taxes. Thus he departed from Bentham, who favored a progressive
income tax. In further support of justice, Mill favored a heavy
inheritance tax, inheritances being unearned by recipients, with
receipts supporting what we might call "universal education" or "a
fair start" for the upcoming generation.

> I hold it therefore the duty of government to give
> pecuniary support to elementary schools, such as
> to render them accessible to the poor, either freely,
> or for a payment too inconsiderable to be sensibly
> felt.[110]

---

[108] Mill, *Principles*, 350. (Book II, chapter 1, §1).

[109] Ibid., 360. (II, 1, 3).

[110] Ibid., 320. (V, 11, 8). Mill never attended school, though his extraordinary
education – tutored by his father, Bentham, and others – is a matter of legend.

He anticipated a variety of schools and curricula, but expected that most children would learn to read, write, and cipher in the lower grades of public schools. While children of well to do families would attend the best of schools, every child would get the chance for an education leading to a more satisfying and even-handed life. Some less advantaged kids would rise like rockets with only this modest boost.

Once educated and employable, people who worked hard or got lucky would get relatively high incomes – to be accepted as fair and just by social convention. If a person could work but didn't, then he or she wouldn't get much income – also a just reward. But if a person could not work, perhaps due to illness, injury, or handicap, then he or she should get modest support under the imperatives of traditional morality.[111]

> ... we may suppose this better distribution of property attained, by the joint effect of the prudence and frugality of individuals, and of a system of legislation favouring equality of fortunes, so far as is consistent with the just claim of the individual to the fruits, whether great or small, of his or her own industry. We suppose, for instance, ..., a limitation of the sum which any one person may acquire by gift or inheritance, to the amount sufficient to constitute a moderate independence.[112]

These were radical proposals. Among other things, they challenged inheritance, the historical standard of distributing work and income by birthright. Born into wealth, a person's income was secure and independent of work. But if born into the working

---

[111] Mill did not appeal in particular to *Noblesse Oblige* or Old Testament prophets to rationalize support for the needy. He preferred to leave moral footings to individual priorities, and he strongly preferred charitable contributions to government transfers.

[112] Mill, *Principles*, 115 (IV, VI, 2).

class, men and women could work very hard and cleverly at their inherited careers but still get little in compensation. Many were born into serfdom, or slavery. Preferring that income correlate with work, Mill challenged the system of birthright, which simply failed the test of justice.

Second, he suggested that everyone pay the same rate of taxes, allowing wealth to accumulate accordingly. Upon death, the wealth of the deceased would be taxed heavily, the proceeds directed toward "fair start" programs - primarily of universal education, but also perhaps for nutrition, health, etc., for children and the genuinely disabled.

Liberty would be expanded as people became free to make a living according to their talents and energies, strengthened by schooling. Income would be more self-determined than under the old system of inheritance. Everyone would enjoy the same rights of speech, religion, etc., including a semblance of "fair start."[113]

Smith had seen schooling as a boon to prosperity and as solution to the problems of boredom and malaise in a world of routine work. Recall his concern:

> The man whose life is spent in performing a few
> simple operations, of which the effects too are,
> perhaps, always the same, ... becomes as stupid
> and ignorant as it is possible for a human creature
> to become.[114]

Mill focused more on fairness, sensing that gains in justice would enhance liberty. Schooling could put a bloom on economic life,

---

[113] For original text, see Mill, *Principles*, 118-141. This is chapter 7 of book IV, "On the Probable Futurity of the Labouring Classes." For orientation, see chapters on Mill in Heilbroner, *Worldly Philosophers* or Ekelund & Hebert, *A History of Economic Theory and Method*.

[114] Smith, *Wealth*, V, 1, 178.

elevate social justice, and boost productivity into the future; for all intents and purposes liberty would grow in a virtuous cycle.[115]

Mill's *Principles* comprised five books with over 600 pages. At the end of Book Five, Mill gives us a chapter entitled "Of the Grounds and Limits of the Laissez-Faire or Non-Interference Principle." He begins that chapter by summarizing objections to government interference, defending laissez-faire as the general rule, and then turns to situations where government intervention seems justified – in nine parts. Not to belabor, he argues in those sections for protections on behalf of children and animals, noting, "The case of women is not analogous." Women, being neither minors nor of lower intelligence, deserved liberty as full-fledged members of political society. Certainly laws should not constrain their freedoms relative to men. He went on to notice legitimate roles of government in the areas of perpetual contracts, length of the working day, poor laws, and so forth. The point here is that Mill recognized many instances where government intervention could be justified in the interest of liberty, justice, and decency.

A staunch advocate of expanding liberty, Mill ended *Principles* with a provocative lament concerning coercion and waste. To wit,

> Even in the best state which society has yet reached, it is lamentable to think how great a proportion of all the efforts and talents in the world are employed in merely neutralizing one another. It is the proper end of government to reduce this wretched waste to the smallest possible amount, by taking such measures as shall cause the energies now spent by mankind in injuring one another, or in protecting themselves against injury, to be turned to the legitimate employment of the human faculties, that of compelling the powers of

---

[115] Material prosperity enhances liberty, maybe expanding it, further stimulating prosperity, etc. See Sen, *Development as Freedom.*

nature to be more and more subservient to physical and moral good.[116]

Surely Mill would be disappointed, but hardly surprised, at today's multi-billion dollar industries of bluster, threat, protection, advocacy, and self-defense. Where is cooperation? Where is sharing? Where are solidarity and tolerance?

Mill's ideas fit well with Scandinavian dispositions and with progressive intellectuals, but they met strong resistance in circles favoring stability and privilege. British neoclassical economists reacted with abstract theorems and statistics to support free trade, free enterprise, laissez-faire, and "efficiency" under a host of assumptions that distracted from issues of justice and distribution.

These days we read John Rawls, Amartya Sen, Ronald Dworkin, Kenneth Arrow, Arthur Okun, Joseph Stiglitz, and others who advocate discussions of distributive justice in the economics curriculum. In a review of Rawls's *Theory of Justice*, for example, Kenneth Arrow writes in a way reminiscent of Mill.

> This generalized difference principle, as Rawls terms it, is no tautology. In particular, it implies that even natural advantages, superiorities of intelligence or strength, do not in themselves create any claims to greater rewards. The principles of justice are 'an agreement to regard the distribution of natural talents as a common asset and to share in the benefits of this distribution.'
>
> "Personally, I share fully this value judgment; and, indeed, it is implied by almost all attempts at full formalization of welfare economics. But a contradictory proposition: that an individual is entitled to what he creates, is widely and unreflectively held; when teaching elementary economics,

---

[116] Mill, *Principles*, 346. (V, 11, 16).

I have had considerable difficulty in persuading the students that this productivity principle was not completely self-evident."[117]

Alas! What exactly are the just desserts of free people in ideal liberty?

---

[117] Kenneth Arrow, "Some Ordinalist-Utilitarian Notes on Rawls's *Theory of Justice*," *The Journal of Philosophy* 70 (1973): 247-248.

CHAPTER 16

The Welfare State and Liberty

"No, I do not think it can."
- Joseph Schumpeter's answer to
   "Can capitalism survive?"

Schumpeter imagined voters stressed by the successes of capitalism picking socialism. Though his image of the socialist alternative remained hazy, a version of his forecast may sit at the doorstep today - with a twist of Mill – widely called the welfare state.

Welfare states share three essential traits: economic nationalism, agreement on a fair or just distribution of income, and consensus on conditions of membership. To elaborate briefly, economic nationalism refers to a shared determination to attain competitive standing in the global economy but with a willingness to protect certain domestic values and industries; fair distribution relates to benefits of citizenship or membership, usually comprising a set of essential goods and services made available to all; and membership involves well defined conditions of belonging, including the process of welcoming newcomers, whether by birth or legal immigration. While there is no particular set of solutions implied, the Scandinavian nations serve well as pattern states, having faced intense global competition with national solidarity for upwards of a century.[118]

First and foremost, the welfare state is a nationalistic enterprise, at least in economic terms. Not wanting to appear isolationist or unconcerned for the plights of others around the world, the Scandinavian nations have actively participated in the United Nations, the WHO, and many ventures on behalf of developing nations. But when it comes to their own economic fortunes, the imperative is to be competitive, their relatively small size implying a high degree of openness to trade (with exports comprising up to 85 percent of GDP). Certain sectors are protected in the national interest (typically agriculture, forestry, and food processing) but most are left unprotected or exposed. Among the open sectors several must emerge as successful exporters lest imports lead to debilitating deficits in trade. A general priority for high productivity in all sectors becomes especially important for export sectors lest they lose their competitive standing in global markets.

As to fairness, all citizens and approved residents should feel a sense of belonging and a corresponding willingness to work and pay taxes. All qualify for the approved array of essential goods and services, usually including health care, retirement benefits, and education through university and graduate school. These benefits and responsibilities of membership help to maintain social cohesion, but two problems remain likely: slackers and paralysis stemming from unresolved domestic conflicts. Best to have everyone employed and productive.

Each welfare state enjoys a modicum of self-determination, typically resolved by constitutional procedures and referenda. All

---

[118] A pattern state in this case refers to a standard for emulation. For example, the United States served as a pattern state for the EU and many free trade agreements. Of the Scandinavian nations, Norway is of particular interest, as its citizens voted not to join the EU in two national referenda, 1972 and 1994. Denmark joined the EU in 1972 following a referendum; Sweden and Finland joined in 1995, also following referenda.

choices are in play, as new challenges and gainful reforms will surely arise.

Finally, the welfare state is no panacea. It requires the capitalistic discipline of energetic saving and clever investment. Slippage on either front can be troublesome. It also requires a lot of tolerance and dispute management.

That said, the American electorate might be ready to evolve for itself a welfare state. Given political divisions, it is a distant possibility, and politicians may not be willing to deliver. So, outlandish though it may seem, this chapter considers the possibility that the American electorate might be ready in Schumpeter's sense to redirect its course in the global economy.

What evidence indicates America's desire to move in this direction? Recent elections offer strong hints. At the local level, for example, several path-breaking ballot initiatives and referenda have been approved in California and Oregon to institute substantial increases in minimum wages, some to $15 and $17 per hour. Many cities and states are likely to follow, addressing issues of fairness key to the construction of a welfare state. More prominently, the national election of 2016 featured Bernie Sanders and Donald Trump emphasizing the three attributes of a prospective welfare state. Hillary Clinton joined a bit late, having previously promoted expanding globalization and its substantial pressures on the national economy.

While all three candidates touted nationalism, membership, and fairness, their campaign rhetoric varied markedly and substantively: Sanders promoted himself as a democratic socialist in the progressive tradition, encouraging immigration reform and trade protection while lamenting the decline of America's middle class; Trump voiced nationalist sentiments with more bluster, often divisively (expel illegal immigrants, keep Muslims out, build a wall, resurrect the middle class, and dump or renegotiate terrible trade agreements). He threatened Clinton, who tried to inspire national unity, tout trade adjustment assistance, and spotlight the idiocy of trickle-down tax cuts. The contrast in rhetoric could hardly be more stark: thoughtful versus visceral, appeals to hope versus the cultivation of fear, and calls for mutual interest versus divisive scapegoating. But the three pillars of a welfare state stood out: economic nationalism, fair distribution, and membership. These are the issues to be resolved.

Trump beat Clinton, and some say that Sanders would have beaten Trump. Either way - whether the winner inspired optimistic progress or catered to disappointment and fear - there is only the way forward. Whether voters responded to a "brighter future together" or to "make America great again," the call was for bounded globalization, better incomes for the middle class, and a clearer definition of who we are. If these issues can be resolved, the next step would be to focus on solidarity, sharing, and competitiveness.

The election left many Americans scratching their heads and frightened. Trump's indictments of Hispanics, Muslims, and Climate Fanatics was hardly the preferred way to unify a nation, though it proved to be a viable election strategy.[119] Subsequent tweets, false assertions, berating of the press, disinformation, and denials of evidence seem problematic to national unity. Perhaps the nation can find solidarity around its constitutional system of checks and balances.

Even if America is ready to evolve for itself a welfare state, many barriers remain. The nation needs to develop a shared identity and more discipline.

Senator Sanders used the term democratic socialism, challenging citizens to rethink their words and positions. In fact, Sanders offered a progressive vision that challenged the nation's predominantly capitalist self-image.

To elaborate, words are important. The ancient Greeks reified them as markers of knowledge and awareness, but also recognized

---

[119] See Edward Glaeser, "The Political Economy of Hatred," *Quarterly Journal of Economics* 121 (2005). This article discusses the game-theoretic logic of political maneuvers like scapegoating and divisiveness, featuring examples from postbellum America and Nazi Germany.

that words often lead to confusion.[120] In the realm of economics Fritz Machlup of Princeton University catalogued hundreds of different meanings for such terms as saving, income, and equilibrium (not to mention capitalism, socialism, and communism) from high caliber economic scholarship. He called those words kaleidoscopic, prone to abrupt changes in message and color, thus inviting semantic confusion. In that context he wondered how economists, politicians, and citizens could have sensible communications. He wrote, "Some people regard exercises in semantics as a waste of time. I consider them useful, if not indispensable, if we care to understand one another."[121]

Americans predominantly identify their economic system as capitalism. Perhaps after eighty years at odds with fascism and communism they came to think of capitalism as theirs to embrace. Whatever the reason, Americans have rallied to the words capitalist, anti-fascist, anti-communist, and anti-socialist. But unless we clarify our terms this can be highly problematic.

What is capitalism? Is America capitalist?

---

[120] Conversing in search of word-based knowledge, Socrates left many powerful neighbors embarrassed and confused, which eventually led to his execution as a public nuisance. See Plato's *Apology*. In another dialog, Plato's *Republic*, chapter 1, Socrates upset the elites of Athens with his dialectical approach, effectively clearing the deck of conventional meanings of "justice." Two thousand years later, taking a cynical perspective to make a similar point, Goethe's Mephistopheles touted words for their capacity to confound, deceive, and hide ignorance. "It's just when sense is missing that a word comes pat and serves one's purpose most conveniently. Words make for splendid disputations and noble systematizations; words are matters of faith; as you'll have heard, one can take no jot nor tittle from a word." (Goethe, *Faust*, lines 1995-2000).

[121] Fritz Machlup, *Essays in Economic Semantics* (Princeton: Princeton University Press, 1963), 3. Economists had by then developed national accounts in large part to establish consistent operational meanings for kaleidoscopic words like income, consumption, saving, investment, unemployment, inflation, etc. The agreed conventions of measurement forced everyone into the same language when constructing budgets or quasi-scientific studies. Not surprisingly, any scientific findings would be synthetic, subject to interpretation according to the measurement conventions that led to them.

We discern two distinct meanings of the term in economic scholarship, one associated with Marx and the other with Friedman.[122] To set things right, Marx essentially coined the term to identify a distinct stage of history when the social surplus was devoted to investment. At its base, the Law of Moses for capitalism was to save and invest. Capitalists would gather the so-called surplus (roughly, profit) and put it to work for another round of production and yet more profit. The name capitalism was devised to emphasize the vanguard force of capital, ever growing and improving with energetic saving and investment.

Co-opting the term, many scholars and most citizens have come to embrace capitalism as the laissez-faire market system. This is what Milton Friedman had in mind as he composed *Capitalism and Freedom,* encouraging his readers to develop a tolerance for free market outcomes. Subsequent apologists continue to carry the torch for markets against other foundational economic institutions, such as central planning, charismatic leadership, or command-and-control dictatorship.

But notice this: whether you follow capitalism ala Marx or Friedman, society's fate is cast. Social self-determination falls victim either to the forces of history (Marx) or the forces of the market (Friedman). Whichever stand you take, your ship is adrift, moving inexorably down current. An alternative is to clarify social goals and strive to achieve them.

As to the matter at hand, America is hardly capitalistic, whether according to Marx or Friedman. Relative to Marx's conception, Americans are not known so much for their determination to save and invest as for their inclination to borrow and consume.[123] And when it comes to tolerance for free markets,

---

[122] Of some interest, the term "capitalism" has fallen from use in economics; you will barely find the word in contemporary textbooks.

[123] Using credit cards, installment loans, and mortgages, Americans have leveraged themselves into cozy restaurants, fancy cars, and ever more sumptuous homes where families of three or four roam amidst four or more bathrooms, three or more garage stalls, mammoth closets, and vaulted ceilings. Investments?

ala Friedman, America has shown a willingness to intervene in the interest of environmental protection, public health, universal education, worker safety, consumer protection, etc., deploying constitutional authority to alter market processes and outcomes.

The welfare state offers a sensible middle way with a dose of national self-determination. It is no panacea, as noted, as it still requires capitalistic discipline to stay ahead in the increasingly competitive global economy.

Adopting the mantle of a welfare state, citizens move at least momentarily beyond awkward confusion into a new world of decision-making and hard work. In short, when enough citizens make the leap from capitalist identity they come to appreciate a fresh degree of self-determination. Of course, opening this door brings new challenges and yet more words: protection, membership, solidarity, and essential goods and services. There will be plenty of ambiguity and hard work ahead.

How open should the national economy be? What sectors should be protected? How can we improve productivity across the board and maintain a competitive edge in trade? Should we allow foreign suppliers to dump products? How about the outflow of factories and capital? Should every citizen get access to health care? Higher education? Retraining? Should we simplify matters with a guaranteed income? These questions were always there, but they seem fresh in the context of striving to build a self-conscious national welfare state.

The recent election hardly portends movement toward a

These homes and cars are bold, durable consumer products. Instead of saving and investing, Americans are borrowing and consuming.

Americans over the past thirty-five years have not been especially active savers. According to data from the United States Department of Commerce the American savings rate fell steadily through the 'Eighties, from 7.5 percent in 1981 to 5.3 percent in 1990, and it lingered at low levels through the Nineties. Since 1994 American households have saved less than five percent of their disposable (after tax) income, the low point coming in the fourth quarter of 2000 at minus .01 percent. (See Council of Economic Advisors, *Economic Indicators*, United States Government Printing Office, a monthly publication).

welfare state. Indeed, we face considerable ambiguity and a high likelihood of tax cuts. Trump won with several main points, but presented in brutish fashion with adolescent hyperbole and provocative tweets that complicate discernment. His key points were probably clear enough: repeal or renegotiate multilateral trade deals, reform health care, expel undocumented aliens, build a wall, bring jobs back to rebuild the middle class, change the rules by which capital flows abroad, and bar Muslims from entry.

We don't know what President Trump or Congress will do. He said what he said; they said what they said – and ambiguity reigns. Surely the Trans-Pacific Partnership will be rejected, and it will make sense to reform the immigration system, perhaps starting with the bill that passed the Senate in 2013. But how about climate change agreements, civil rights, and the treatment of Dreamers? Is compassion manifest? These matters relate to social solidarity, but for now the overall picture is hazy and the world is in motion as usual.

Significant challenges lay ahead. Innovations like self-driving vehicles, artificial intelligence, robots, and drones are likely to destroy millions of old jobs even as they create millions of new and different jobs. To take the most conspicuous example, self-driving trucks will carry long-distance loads 24-7, no coffee breaks, no rest stops, and fewer accidents. This will undermine an array of jobs for truckers, taxi drivers, waitresses, cooks, and back office staff.

What to do? One possibility is featherbedding; another is to slow the process of adoption, perhaps phasing with retirements. Retraining will be especially important; some displaced workers will find jobs in programming, logistics, or maintenance of the new fleet. Other displaced workers will find employment in short-haul delivery or driving buses; but most will be steered to viable careers in health care, business, and human and community services.

Whatever happens, investment will be important. Many readers will be surprised to learn that Switzerland leads the world in capital per worker, followed by Luxemburg, Norway, Finland,

Japan, and Sweden. Intent on competitiveness, these countries have made investment and productivity growth drumbeats of their systems.

America has focused on consumption rather than productive investment for upwards of four decades. She has fallen behind many countries in capital per worker, now at roughly half of the Swiss measure. Luckily foreigners have made substantial investments in America, shortening supply chains and hiring available labor.

Related to competitiveness is education, a form of investment, but here too we find telling signs of America's slippage from productive discipline. In 1989 the Educational Testing Service announced the results of a study that compared public school students in six countries: Britain, Canada, Ireland, South Korea, Spain, and the United States. The expectation prior to the study was that American students would stand tall in this competition, but somewhat surprisingly the American students finished last in math scores. South Korea came in first (with an average score of 568); then came the English-speaking provinces of Canada (514-543), Spain (512), Britain (510), Ireland (504), French-speaking Ontarians of Canada (482), and finally the Americans (474). The result was called "sobering."

One needn't wonder how American kids might have fared relative to Japanese, German, or Scandinavian students at the time. That would have been even more embarrassing. True to form, American kids were consuming instead of investing, watching TV, playing games, and enjoying fast food. Meanwhile their lean and hungry counterparts around the world were busy learning calculus, physics, chemistry, statistics, etc., preparing to work for much less than Americans could fathom. And students face more distractions today: cell phones, virtual reality, and social media.

With consumption in the driver's seat, things continued to slip. The Educational Testing Service replicated its study in 1991 and 1995 with even more sobering results. America's ranking on the math test fell to thirteenth among fourteen nations (below

Korea, Russia, Slovenia, and Spain) and twelfth on the science test. The average score on the math test in 1995 ranged from 643 in Singapore to 487 in Spain. The American eighth graders scored 500, forty points behind the average scores of eighth graders in Slovenia and Bulgaria.

In 2001 New York City schools began hiring math and science teachers from the Czech Republic, Slovakia, Hungary, and other Eastern European countries. The New York schools had to go abroad for teachers!

America's slip in educational discipline has come alongside an alarming pattern of disinvestment, including drug abuse, smoking, physical inactivity, and wasted time. This pattern is antithetical to capitalism and successful welfare states; instead of saving and investing, our kids are consuming and vandalizing.

So if you think of America as capitalistic, think again. The capitalistic discipline of saving and investing began slipping long ago, and it will take time and effort to recover. If a welfare state appears to be the answer, be sure that it will require investment and hard work. The welfare state is no panacea.

As to imagining a fair distribution for America, the $15 per hour wage is a good start for productive labor, especially in dynamic urban areas. It is practical and distinct, even if it reduces profit and toys with the classic wage-price spiral. Going further toward a fair distribution, the Affordable Care Act was a step in the right direction, but stalled in improvements by an obstructionist Congress. It or something close will probably persist. Meanwhile, many candidates proposed free tuition for students progressing in higher education or career training. Retraining opportunities also enhance fairness for optimistic and determined workers.

Given the tenor of political rhetoric, beware of equality as a goal or inequality as an enemy; that is ridiculous and impractical. Equality may be important in mathematics, but it makes little sense in the social sciences, mainly due to widespread incommensurability: no two people are alike; no two towns are alike; no two houses are alike; regions vary; and no two automobiles provide the same satisfaction. Things simply do not add up. What set of goods and services could possibly constitute equality? What could it possibly mean to have equal incomes, equal educations, or equal levels of happiness? What is equal health?

The sensible way to proceed is to pick a set of essential goods and services to be made available to all. Day care, medical care, schooling, housing, access to good food and water, retirement benefits, training opportunities, and unemployment benefits are typical. The Earned Income Tax Credit might be expanded. Children must be well resourced; they are the future.

Once everyone is availed of an agreed array of essential goods and services, every household is on its own, free to compete, its liberty and capacities augmented by a well-resourced start and ready support.

CONCLUSION

Against a backdrop of conventional wisdom that matches liberty with small government, this essay has found complexity by exploring connections between liberty and laissez-faire. A simple Venn diagram framed the discussion, highlighting four categories of social circumstance, the first being the coincidence of liberty and laissez-faire, touted by economists who appreciate the "beauty" of market mechanics and self-managed systems. But laissez-faire can also pair with coercion and oppression as exemplified by racism, sexism, and religious persecution. Turning from laissez-faire to government intervention, we found the somewhat tarnished coincidence of government and liberty (emancipation, civil rights legislation, and freedoms of speech, press, and religion), and instances where constitutional governments have oppressed (witness slavery, Jim Crow, abusive treatment of indigenous people, racial profiling, and concentration camps).

Citizens who value liberty must be alert to all these possibilities as a matter of civic duty and personal enlightenment. The challenge is to surmount conventional wisdom in the quest for higher ground.[124] In fact, there is no simple rule of thumb to de-

---

[124] The venerable Immanuel Kant noted that most people take lethargic refuge in simple agreement with others, conforming in view rather than working to discern their own stands. He called such conformity "nonage" (acting as a minor instead of an adult), characterizing it as lazy, weak, and cowardly; and he implored people to judge for themselves based on personal experience, responsible study, and independent contemplation. "Dare to know! Have the courage to use your own understanding." Immanuel Kant, "What is Enlightenment?" *Berlin Monthly*, December 1784.

termine the optimal size of government for the sake of liberty. Among other things the ideal size will depend on culture, market performance, economic and political philosophies, social cohesion, historical circumstance, and the prevailing sense of justice.

This essay has highlighted circumstances and questions faced by alert citizens as they shape government in the interest of liberty. Rather than pontificating, it has summarized eminent but competing answers - on grounds that people are better equipped with unanswered questions than with unquestioned answers.

Reviewing main themes, first is that laissez-faire in the economic realm of production and consumption has contributed hugely to human prosperity and freedom. The benefits have included a wealth of rewarding jobs and welcome products for the wardrobe, kitchen, and garage - putting an unprecedented bloom on growing liberty. But the outcomes of laissez-faire do not weave into a constant cloth; free enterprise has also generated unwelcome outcomes in terms of health, debt, safety, environmental quality, discrimination, and disappointment. Some enterprises are outright criminal. All things considered, laissez-faire routinely leaves a residue of significant problems for which citizens have found varying levels of relief through government. The result is a mixed economic and social system with markets and governments as instruments of freedom and prosperity.

Searching venerable scholarship, we have sampled a galaxy of eminent thinkers and their insights. Some have favored interventionist policies, as with Mill's fair start and Stern's carbon tax. Others have favored policy repeal or reform, especially aiming at regulatory schemes, as when Friedman complained of rent control, farm subsidies, and licensure. But even Friedman, perhaps the most convincing of liberal voices in support of laissez-faire (recall "unanimity and nonconformity"), could support public efforts to assist the poor and destitute. That said, he like Mill preferred that most such support come from the grass roots.[125]

---

[125] In his introduction to *Capitalism and Freedom*, page 5, Friedman wished to be called a "liberal," but knew the label to have been co-opted. As to redistribution,

This essay has noted tools available for gainful intervention, including cleverly targeted taxes, subsidies, transfers, credit controls, regulation, and deregulation. Wisdom suggests keeping all options open.

Citizens cannot escape the obligation to study, contemplate, and take positions in a constitutional system of governance. "We the People" must strive for a more perfect union; and no one said it would be easy. Once goals are set, policy design and reform pose difficult challenges, and wisdom suggests that informed citizens maintain a suspicious disposition to defend against the proliferation of bad ideas. As a rule of thumb, watch for proposals that match well with the decentralized system of markets, and beware of proposals that offer little more than platitudes – though they attract a throng.

Given perceived advantages of laissez-faire markets, economists suggest a general preference for tax or subsidy incentives over regulation, thinking that direct controls constitute a scarce resource to be used only in relatively dire situations such as the poisoning of reservoirs or aquifers. Thus, when it came to removing lead from automotive fuels, economists preferred an additional tax on leaded gasoline to drive it off the market – a tax that would leave people free to decide whether to use unleaded gasoline. That said, politicians rule according to the constitution; economists only advise.

Moving from the national to the international realm, a significant problem arises with the absence of a global government. This situation will persist so long as established nations dissent from global confederation, thus stalling policies to address international problems like human trafficking, drug trade, climate change, sea rise, pollution, and war. Recent anti-global sentiment as expressed by Brexit, the election of Mr. Trump, and the rise of reactionary

see his chapter "The Alleviation of Poverty," 190-195, where Friedman expressed his preference for private charities, but that he could support a tax and transfer scheme owing to "neighborhood effects" and free riders. There he famously proposed a "negative income tax."

dispositions may foretell increased difficulty in the progress of global problem solving.

Nations that resist global governance invariably worry about the imposition of non-local values: the US may not want German discipline or high taxes on fossil fuel; China may not want American permissiveness; Iraq may not want universal or Western education; and so on, and so forth. It is hard for nations to reconcile their variations of tradition and routine, and as with any diverse citizenry their bickering often precludes mutually beneficial cooperation. Meanwhile, laissez-faire emerges by default with attending problems of xenophobia, bigotry, global warming, pollution, and massive migrations.

Looking back, we have sampled contributions from economics, law, sociology, history, political science, and philosophy. Orienting to liberty, we have found laissez-faire and government in creative tension, the Yin and Yang of libertarian aspiration.

APPENDIX - BIOGRAPHIES

This appendix elaborates briefly on a group of venerable economists who have stood out in the discussion of liberty and laissez-faire. It is something of an embarrassment that no women are recognized. In fact, women have been around and involved: Maria Edgeworth, Harriet Mill, and Joan Robinson come quickly to mind, but their notable contributions arose tangential to the topic at hand. It is also safe to say that women have faced systemic barriers as scholars. More recently, women have risen in the ranks of social economics with contributions to our topic. Nancy Folbre joined the Stiglitz Commission in assessing GDP as a measure of national welfare, for example, and Deirdre McKloskey has criticized regulatory policies and emphasized the importance of ideas to economic development.

This set of sketches covers nine men who dominate in the history of economic and social thought. All departed, each was a versatile, multi-faceted scholar with an interesting biography. Readers are encouraged to dig deeper into their lives, times, and ideas.

We begin with venerable contributors to classical political economy: Smith, Malthus, Ricardo, and Marx. Each imagined an unfolding pattern of history yet ahead, but before Darwin had enunciated his theory of evolution. Thus we have pre-Darwinian thinkers contemplating trajectories with a mindset from physics, logic, and cosmology.

Adam Smith (1723-1790)

Smith imagined a "system of natural liberty" or "perfect liberty" to replace what he called "the mercantile system" of his day. His new system would be more productive, based on freedom, competition, and leadership by consumers whose standard of living constituted a nation's true wealth.

Smith was Professor of Moral Philosophy at the University of Glasgow and a beloved teacher. He was also known as something of a scatterbrain, occasionally slipping into reveries and thoughtful digressions. A student of Francis Hutchinson and friend of David Hume, Smith was a mainstay in the Scotish Enlightenment, writing two important books: *Theory of Moral Sentiments* and *Wealth of Nations*.

Thomas Robert Malthus (1766-1834)

Malthus proposed a dire prospect for the natural order: a rising population pushing against the earth's carrying capacity. This would tend to put most of society at or near the edge of starvation with population checks at play: war, disease, pestilence, hunger, and misery. Yet he was a kind man, loving and pastoral, an Anglican Priest and professional economist. His *Essay on Population* would influence Darwin. Digging deeper, readers will find Malthus an interesting character, challenged with a cleft lip but encouraged by his father to be creative and honest. His famous debates with Ricardo on the distribution of rents to the landed class became a metaphor for modern discussions on the relationship between economic contribution and income.

David Ricardo (1772-1823)

Ricardo was a brilliant businessman and close friend of Malthus who gathered up a great fortune before becoming a Member of Parliament. A strong advocate of free trade and laissez-faire, his theories of distribution and comparative advantage were based on his idea of falling marginal product, still a mainstay of economic theory. His writings, gathered into eleven volumes by Professor Sraffa at Cambridge University, include a massive correspondence with Malthus. Also of note, Ricardo's theory of distribution strongly influenced Marx, who reduced the number of "constituent classes" from three to two, lopping off the landlord class as pre-capitalist. Thus Marx proceeded with just two classes, the Bourgeoisie (owners) and the Proletariat (workers).

Karl Marx (1818-1883)

Marx proposed a system called capitalism, named for its trait of directing society's surplus to investment. The penchant to accumulate capital implied an accelerating capacity to produce commodities by consuming the finite world of resources.

Marx saw capitalism as an era of history destined to generate unprecedented material prosperity, but with episodes of tension and crisis featuring a business cycle, advertising, growing productivity, ideology, confusion, and eventually revolution. His massive economic treatise was *Das Kapital*, completed by his dashing friend and colleague Friedrich Engels.

Marx himself was decidedly otherworldly. Always in financial straits, he couldn't find his way to a steady income; his beloved family often went to bed hungry; and he rarely had money for a new pair of shoes. Things got so bad one year that his wife Jenny, herself from an aristocratic German family, had to beg neighbors for money to buy a casket in which to bury their deceased son.

Most people associate Marx with the Soviet Union, but neither the logic nor the heavy-handedness of the Soviets came from Karl Marx. He himself was an activist philosopher, reprobate, and family man who espoused secular humanism. A progressive German intellectual and a refugee of the German police state, he worked most of his life in Britain mainly on the labor theory of value and the dialectics of history. He offered little insight into the practical details of making nuts and bolts or holding inventories of spare parts. He wrote virtually nothing about the complex interconnections of making barrels, staves, flour, bread, wheels, shoes, plumbing fixtures, sewers, axles, and handles. He never imagined carburetors, fighter planes, or power brakes. In short, he was a most unhelpful choice to support Soviet central planning.

John Stuart Mill (1806-1873).

And then there was Mill, a utilitarian, bridging the classical and the neoclassical schools of economics. Influenced by his father, James Mill, and his father's friends - Bentham, Ricardo, and Malthus - he stood tall and alone, but for his beloved wife Harriet and daughter Helen. His stern intellectual upbringing almost drove him crazy, but luckily it did not.

Next came neoclassical economists, offering a purely logical portrait of the market system by way of axioms and theorems. Its approach to people and history would be via calculus and differential equations. Accordingly, if a person had positive and declining marginal utility for each and every good, then her demand for each good would be inversely related to its price, other things equal. And so it goes, an assembly of valid arguments moving from presumptions to conclusions (axioms to theorems), depicting the mechanics of idealized markets. An early version was called psychophysics, highly mathematical and explicitly connected to Newtonian mechanics via calculus.

The "beauty" of neoclassical economic thought (textbook economics today) relates to its formal elegance. If the axioms are true, then the conclusions must be true, per validity. All the arguments are valid. And even if the axioms aren't true, the conclusions might still be true. What cannot happen is for the axioms to be true and the conclusions false. It is an elegant edifice of pure thought.

Ponder Figure 9 from a graduate student's notebook. The excerpt concerns the first theorem of welfare economics, that an ideal competitive equilibrium will be efficient, using a line of reasoning called *reductio ad absurdum*.

Figure 9.

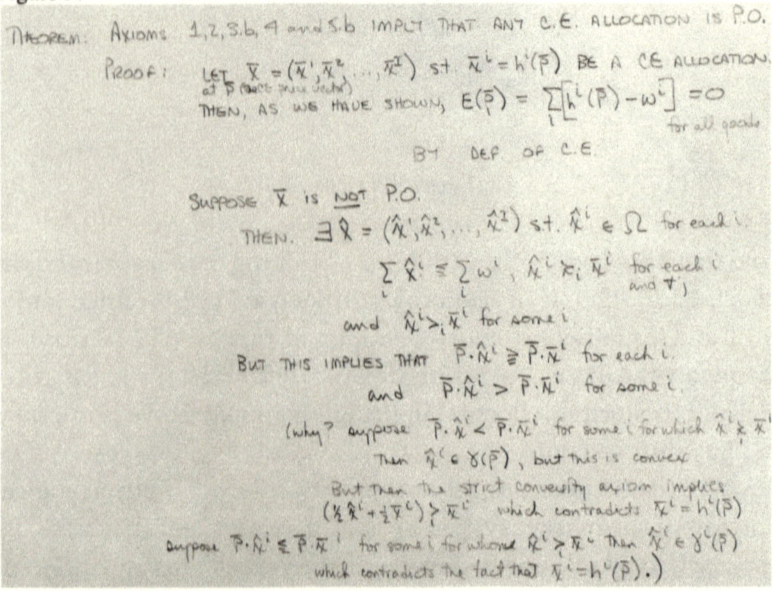
THEOREM: AXIOMS 1, 2, 3.b, 4 and 5.b IMPLY THAT ANY C.E. ALLOCATION IS P.O.

PROOF: LET $\bar{x} = (\bar{x}^1, \bar{x}^2, \ldots, \bar{x}^I)$ s.t. $\bar{x}^i = h^i(\bar{p})$ BE A CE ALLOCATION. at $\bar{p}$ (exact price vector)

THEN, AS WE HAVE SHOWN, $E(\bar{p}) = \sum_i [h^i(\bar{p}) - \omega^i] = 0$ for all goods

BY DEF OF C.E.

SUPPOSE $\bar{x}$ is NOT P.O.

THEN. $\exists \hat{x} = (\hat{x}^1, \hat{x}^2, \ldots, \hat{x}^I)$ s.t. $\hat{x}^i \in \Omega$ for each i.

$\sum_i \hat{x}^i \leq \sum_i \omega^i$, $\hat{x}^i \succsim_i \bar{x}^i$ for each i and $\forall_i$)

and $\hat{x}^i \succ_i \bar{x}^i$ for some i

BUT THIS IMPLIES THAT $\bar{p} \cdot \hat{x}^i \geqq \bar{p} \cdot \bar{x}^i$ for each i.

and $\bar{p} \cdot \hat{x}^i > \bar{p} \cdot \bar{x}^i$ for some i.

(why? suppose $\bar{p} \cdot \hat{x}^i < \bar{p} \cdot \bar{x}^i$ for some i for which $\hat{x}^i \succsim_i \bar{x}^i$

Then $\hat{x}^i \in \gamma(\bar{p})$, but this is convex

But then the strict convexity axiom implies

$(\frac{1}{2}\hat{x}^i + \frac{1}{2}\bar{x}^i) \succ_i \bar{x}^i$ which contradicts $\bar{x}^i = h^i(\bar{p})$

suppose $\bar{p} \cdot \hat{x}^i \leqq \bar{p} \cdot \bar{x}^i$ for some i for whom $\hat{x}^i \succ_i \bar{x}^i$ then $\hat{x}^i \in \gamma^i(\bar{p})$

which contradicts the fact that $\bar{x}^i = h^i(\bar{p})$.)

Clearly economic theory can get to look pretty ridiculous, but it has redeeming features for those who stick with it.

Moving to the twentieth century, this appendix features four who stand out for their breadth of vision. Each has a Renaissance reputation and fascinating bio that exceed the scope of this project. The notes below will be brief and germane.

August Friedrich von Hayek (1899-1992)

Friedrich Hayek grew up in Austria and studied at the University of Vienna, a hot bed of positivist philosophy at the time. The son of a professor and second cousin to Wittgenstein, Hayek operated in an environment saturated with energetic examinations of science and mathematics, including the famous Vienna Circle. Returning from war as a decorated soldier, Hayek completed his doctorate of law in 1921 and a second doctorate in political science two years later. Then he joined a group of gifted friends in a private seminar facilitated by Ludwig von Mises himself. It is hard to imagine a more fertile environment for a young intellectual.

The seminar was wide-ranging, but Hayek became focused on

money and business cycles. His work soon caught the attention of scholars at the London School of Economics, and Hayek accepted a position there in 1931. He quickly extended his research in economics, but also paid special attention to developments in Germany that were highly regarded by bureaucrats in Britain and the United States. Hitler was partnering with industry to achieve social goals. Overlooking the successes of fascist "corporatism," Hayek focused on the rise of the totalitarian state. His political and economic writing converged to warn about the danger posed by National Socialism versus decentralized markets – even in times of depression. Such is the origin of *Road to Serfdom*.

He and his fellow Austrian, Karl Popper, the famous philosopher of science, became colleagues at the London School - each anxious about by what they called "scientism." Both doubted the efficacy of using methods from the natural sciences for explorations in the social sciences, though both deeply appreciated the self-organizing ecology of markets.

Having risen into the highest ranks of professional economists, Hayek was recruited to the University of Chicago where he became Professor of Social and Moral Sciences in 1950. By the time he left Chicago in 1962 he was regarded as the world's preeminent libertarian economist, having published *The Constitution of Liberty* in addition to a host of respected papers and books. He was awarded the Nobel Prize in 1974 with Gunnar Myrdal for his work in monetary economics, business cycles, and institutions.

Harvard University, Harvard University Archives, W351238_1

Joseph Alois Schumpeter (1883-1950)
HUGBS 276.90, olvwork351238, Harvard University Archives

Also Austrian, Schumpeter studied at the University of Vienna
with a focus on law and economics, and he too was quickly recognized for his academic acumen. He taught for a while at Graz,
published *The Theory of Economic Development* in 1911 (translated
to English in 1934), and then turned to a stint in government, rising in 1919 to the position of Minister of Finance. He then moved
to academic positions, starting at the University of Bonn. Anxious
over the rise of Hitler, he left Germany and settled permanently
in the United States upon accepting a position as professor of economics at Harvard University in 1932.

He was a determined scholar, deeply committed to the study
of economic development, business cycles, and the history of economic thought; he published and taught with energy and aplomb.
He is best known for a trade book, *Capitalism, Socialism, and
Democracy*, featuring the terms entrepreneur and creative destruction. He was a strong advocate of free markets, but from a

dynamic perspective that led him to prefer monopoly to perfect competition. His view of history emphasized great men, which clearly bled into his economics via entrepreneurs who inject progressive disturbances into the system of markets that might otherwise adjust toward a steady state. Schumpeter stands out today for his dynamic view of markets versus the static dogma of orthodoxy.

Gunnar Myrdal (1898-1987)
Upsala Nya Tidning, Uppsala, Sweden

Myrdal was a Swedish scholar and politician, trained in mathematics, economics, sociology, and anthropology, and known as a creative researcher and activist. He graduated from Stockholm University with a law degree, and took his doctorate in economics four years later, strongly influenced by Knut Wicksell, also broadbased and politically active.

Myrdal became professor at the Stockholm School of Economics in 1933, and that same year became a Member of Parliament. He remained active in Swedish politics, serving in many posts, including minister of trade and commerce. He had by then published a seminal work on countercyclical monetary and fiscal policy, four years before Keynes, and some have speculated that had he published in English rather than Swedish, he would have elbowed Keynes in the field. As it turned out he gained unusual notoriety for his study of racial tensions in America, a project that he started in 1938. His book *An American Dilemma* was published in 1944, a stunning success that would influence the Supreme Court's decision in Brown v Board of Education.

Myrdal moved back and forth between academe and public service. His wide range of scholarship made him a key figure in the development of the Swedish welfare state, and his book *Beyond the Welfare State* (1960) looked ahead with an amalgam of views from politics, economics, sociology, history, and ethics.

He was awarded the Nobel Prize in Economic Science with Friedrich Hayek in 1974. The Nobel Committee cited their "pioneering work in the theory of money and economic fluctuations and their penetrating analysis of the interdependence of economic, social and institutional phenomenon." Of related interest, Myrdal and his wife Alva - both politicians – contributed significantly as humanitarians in the promotion of economic development, for which she was awarded the Nobel Peace Prize in 1982. Finally, Myrdal labeled fellow economists of conservative stripe – notably Hayek and Friedman - as "reactionaries," for which he will also be remembered.

Milton Friedman (1912-2006)

Friedman knew both Mises and Hayek, and considered himself the most flexible of the three. That said, Friedman was not known for his flexibility, but for his dogged and tenacious style of discourse.

Called "the most influential economist of the second half of the 20th century," one is left to imagine Keynes taking at least the first half. But Friedman's influence continues almost unabated into the 21st century, a champion of free markets and monetarism.

Friedman completed his undergraduate studies in economics and mathematics at Rutgers, earned his MA at the University of Chicago in 1932 and his PhD from Columbia University in 1946. In the meanwhile he studied statistics with Harold Hotelling, taught at UW-Madison and Minnesota, worked for the federal government and the Bureau of Economic Research, and came to take firm positions against price controls and discretionary monetary policy.

He accepted a teaching position at the University of Chicago in 1946, remaining there for 30 years as pillar of a department noted for its interpretations of data and advocacy of free markets.

He won the Nobel Prize in 1976 for research in monetary theory, consumption, and the complexities of public policy. But for all his research and publications, his greatest influence may be in conservative political philosophy, as politicians and citizens resonated to his message of laissez-faire. Barry Goldwater, Ronald Reagan, Margaret Thatcher, and Alan Greenspan appreciated his wisdom, as have Eastern European leaders since 1991 and contemporary American conservatives like Rand Paul and Paul Ryan. Friedman's influence stems largely from his 1962 publication, *Capitalism and Freedom*, advocating deregulation, floating exchange rates, school vouchers, a volunteer army, and the negative income tax. He continued delivering his message into retirement with PBS and the Free to Choose Network. He supported libertarian causes from gay rights and legalized marijuana to reforms of social security.

SUGGESTED RESOURCES AND READINGS

The people and terms referenced in this primer have attracted considerable coverage on the web, allowing readers to enjoy the intersection of biography, history, and ideas via surfing. Consider starting with Adam Smith, Jeremy Bentham, or conspicuous consumption. Read and link, as usual, but try to linger on each item – fighting impatience.

Among web-based resources, find lectures and interviews on YouTube. Start by searching for vignettes featuring Milton Friedman with his optimistic view of the market system. Also enjoy Adam Smith, Thomas Malthus, Friedrich Hayek, Thomas Sowell, John Rawls, Kenneth Arrow, etc. In addition, much of the classic literature on economics and liberty, searchable, is on the web at the Library of Economics and Liberty. Another germane online resource is the Library of Liberty. Most items in the bibliography to follow are available on the web.

Among the best empirical portraits of the social universe, Hans Rosling's *Gapminder* is available for download. Also find many of his presentations on YouTube.

Suggested Readings:

For a general audience, including teens, the following 14 items (often only a single chapter or section) can deepen awareness of issues raised in this essay.

The United States Constitution
> The Constitution frames contemporary American society, establishing its rule of law. Citizens are presumed to have sworn allegiance to it, at least tacitly, but in fact few have studied it or expressed a formal oath. It is available on the Internet.
>
> Also available on the Internet are the Federalist Papers, written by Alexander Hamilton, James Madison, and John Jay to encourage adoption of the Constitution. The papers are collectively ranked among the most important works of American political philosophy.

Aristotle. *Nicomachean Ethics.* Oxford: Oxford University Press, 1990.
> Especially Book IV, "Virtues Concerned with Money," Sections 1 and 2, "Liberality" and "Magnificence," respectively. Aristotle wrote this book for his son Nicomachus.

Banfield, Edward. *The Unheavenly City Revisited.* Prospect Heights, Illinois: Waveland Press, Inc., 1975. Especially chapter one, "Introduction."
> Banfield was a highly respected political scientist at Harvard and Chicago before joining the Nixon administration as domestic advisor to the President. This book aroused considerable criticism, but stands today as a clear conservative statement on limited federal spending and leaving more burdens at the door of state and local finance.

Beckerman, Wilfred. *Economics as Applied Ethics.* London: Palgrave Macmillan, 2011.
> This book surveys welfare economics for readers with a modest orientation to microeconomics. It

departs from theory to related issues of ethics and policy.

Friedman, Milton. *Capitalism and Freedom.* Chicago: Chicago University Press, 1962.
> This is Friedman's classic. Read it and wonder. Many have found it compelling as a case against government intervention in general.

Galbraith, John Kenneth. *The Affluent Society.* New York: Houghton Mifflin, 1957.
> Galbraith was an influential public intellectual and professor of economics at Harvard, tall and dapper. He served as Price Administrator under President Roosevelt and Ambassador to India during the Kennedy Administration. An admirer of Veblen, he wrote extensively and clearly, including *The Affluent Society*, one of the few best sellers in economics.

Heilbroner, Robert. *The Worldly Philosophers,* 7th Ed. New York: Simon & Schuster, 1995.
> This highly readable introduction to economics invites readers to a stimulating combination of biography, history, and ideas.

Jane Jacobs, *Cities and The Wealth of Nations.* New York: Random House, 1984.
> Jacobs provides an iconoclastic view of economics, arguing that cities and networks of cities (not nations) are the world's salient macroeconomic entity. Arguing her case, she offers an alternative economic geography with five forces that emanate from cities in idiosyncratic ways to create supply regions, transplant regions, and abandoned

regions. Written with a Schumpeterian attitude, this book offers a refreshing voice in the tradition of evolutionary economics.

Okun, Arthur, *Equality and Efficiency.* Washington, DC: Brookings, 1975.
> Okun began service as Chair for President Johnson's Council of Economic Advisors at the age of 40, hence his acquaintance with the War on Poverty. This book came afterward, reflecting on the importance of the market system but also the priority for a more equal sharing of economic prosperity. The best-known element of this book is the "leaky bucket experiment" whereby Okun challenges his reader with an exercise in values clarification (91-95).

Pope Francis. *Evangelii Gaudium.* Rome: Vatican Press, 2013. Esp. chapter 2, paragraphs 52-60.
> Francis challenges market capitalism for lack of a moral orientation to human misery. The brief excerpt from chapter 2 of this encyclical raised a considerable stir; some critics going so far as to call Francis a Marxist, a communist, and unhinged. More important, it represents the deontological approach to assessment (as opposed to the teleo- logical or consequential approach of economics).

Rand, Ayn & Brandon, Nathaniel. *The Virtue of Selfishness.* New York: New American Library, 1961.
> Ayn Rand was co-founder of a school of philos- ophy called Objectivism and an inspirational leader for many libertarians of anarchistic bent. A Russian immigrant to the United States follow- ing the Russian Revolution, she distills her social

philosophy in part against the backdrop of Soviet propaganda, oppression, and central planning. Her most famous books are *Atlas Shrugged* and *The Fountainhead*, highly readable and somewhat polemic. This volume is a compilation of philosophical articles from a journal, *The Objectivist*.

Schultze, Charles L. *The Public Use of Private Interest*. Washington, DC: Brookings, 1976.

Having served as Professor of Economics and Director of the Budget Bureau, Schultz gave the Godkin Lectures at Harvard University in 1976, prior to becoming Chair of President Carter's Council of Economic Advisors. This book presents his lectures on the paradoxical use by lawmakers of command and control regulatory policies to improve upon the market system. He outlines his plan to replace regulations with incentive type systems.

Smith, Adam. *Theory of Moral Sentiments*. London: A Millar, 1759.

Especially Part I, Section 1, Chapter 1 ("Of Sympathy"); and Part IV, Section I, Paragraphs 6-8 (including "The poor man's son"). These readings will give some flavor of Smith's effort to explain morality in natural terms. These readings are popular today in the neurosciences, as they anticipate by centuries "sympathetic brain response."

Smith, Adam. *Wealth of Nations*. London: Methuen & Co., Ltd. 1776.

Especially Book I, Chapter 1, "Of the Division of Labor." Also notice Book 1, Chapter 2, where we find the famous line "It is not from the benevolence of the butcher, the brewer, or the baker, that we expect our dinner, but from their regard to their own interest." We might note however that dinner was rarely served by butchers, brewers, or bakers – but generally by women of the household.

BIBLIOGRAPHY

Alvaredo, Facundo, Atkinson, Anthony, Piketty, Thomas, & Saez, Emmanuel. "The Top 1% in International and Historical Perspective." *Journal of Economic Perspectives* 27, no. 3 (2013): 3-20.

Aristotle. *Nicomachean Ethics*. Oxford: Oxford University Press, 1990.

Arrow, Kenneth. "A Difficulty in the Concept of Social Welfare." *The Journal of Political Economy* 58, no. 4 (1950): 328-346.

Arrow, Kenneth. "Some Ordinalist-Utilitarian Notes on Rawls's Theory of Justice." *The Journal of Philosophy* 70, no. 9 (1973): 245-263.

Banfield, Edward. *The Unheavenly City Revisited*. Prospect Heights, Illinois: Waveland Press, 1975.

Beckerman, Wilfred. *Economics as Applied Ethics*. London: Palgrave Macmillan, 2011.

Bentham, Jeremy. *An Introduction to the Principles of Morals and Legislation*. Oxford: Clarendon Press, 1781.

Broadway, Robin W. and Bruce, Neil. *Welfare Economics*. Oxford: Basil Blackwell, 1984.

Burke, Edmund. *Reflections on the Revolution in France*. New York: Holt, Rinehart and Winston, Dover Edition, 2006.

Chronicle of the Catholic Church in Lithuania (1972-1989). A series of underground pamphlets distributed by dissidents during Soviet times. They were assembled into volumes, now available on the Internet.

Clark, Gregory. *A Farewell to Alms*. Princeton: Princeton University Press, 2007.

Coase, Ronald. "The Problem of Social Cost." *The Journal of Law and Economics* 3 (October, 1960): 1-44.

Daniels, Norman, Kennedy, Bruce, and Kawachi, Ichiro. *Is Inequality Bad for Our Health?* Boston: Beacon Press, 2000.

Davis, Devra. *When Smoke Ran Like Water, Tales of Environmental Deception and the Battle Against Pollution*. New York: Basic Books, 2002.

Ekelund, Robert and Hébert, Robert. *A History of Economic Theory and Method,* 5th Ed. Long Grove, Illinois: Waveland, 2007.

Ellman, Michael, and Kontorovich, Vladimir, Eds. *The Destruction of the Soviet System*. New York: M.E. Sharpe, 1998.

Frank, Robert and Cook, Philip. *The Winner-Take-All Society*. New York: Penguin, 1995.

Friedman, Milton. *Capitalism and Freedom*. Chicago: Chicago University Press, 1962.

Gilkey, Langdon. *Creationism on Trial*. Charlottesville: University of Virginia Press, 1985.

Gintis, Herbert. "A Radical Analysis of Welfare Economics and Individual Development." *Quarterly Journal of Economics* 86, no. 4 (1972): 572-599

Glaeser, Edward. "The Political Economy of Hatred." *Quarterly Journal of Economics* 121, no. 1 (2005). 45-86.

Glaeser, Edward. *Triumph of the City*. New York: Penguin, 2011.

Haidt, Jonathan. *The Righteous Mind, why good people are divided by politics and religion*. New York: Vintage Books, 2012.

Harberger, Arnold. "Monopoly and Resource Allocation," *The American Economic Review* 44, no. 2 (1954). 77-87.

Hayek, Friedrich. "The Use of Knowledge in Society," *American Economic Review* 35, no. 4 (1945): 519-530.

Hayek, Friedrich. *The Road to Serfdom*. Chicago: University of Chicago Press, 2007.

Hayek, Friedrich. *Constitution of Liberty*. Chicago: University of Chicago Press, 1960.

Heilbroner, Robert. *The Worldly Philosophers,* 7th Ed. New York: Simon & Schuster, 1995.

Heilbroner, Robert. *Teachings From The Worldly Philosophy.* New York: W.W. Norton, 1997.

Hirschman, Albert. *Exit, Voice, and Loyalty.* Cambridge: Harvard University Press, 1970.

Hirschman, Albert. *Shifting Involvements, Private Interest and Public Action.* Princeton: Princeton University Press, 1982.

Jacobs, Jane. *Cities and The Wealth of Nations.* New York: Vintage Books, 1984.

Kant, Immanuel. "What is Enlightenment? First published in *Berlin Monthly (Berlinische Monatsschrift)*, December, 1784.

Johnasson, Per-Olov. *An Introduction to Modern Welfare Economics.* Cambridge: Cambridge University Press, 1991.

Landreth, Harry and Colander, David. *History of Economic Thought.* 4th Ed. Mason, Ohio: South-Western, 2001.

Lange, Oskar. "On the Economic Theory of Socialism," *Review of Economic Studies* 4, no. 1 (1936): 53-71.

Lange, Oskar. "On the Economic Theory of Socialism, Part Two," *Review of Economic Studies* 4, no. 2 (1937): 123-142.

Machlup, Fritz. *Essays in Economic Semantics.* Princeton: Princeton University Press, 1963.

Malthus, Thomas. *Essay on the Principle of Population.* New York: Dover, 2007. First published anonymously.

Mandeville, Bernard. *Fable of the Bees: or, Private Vices, Publick Benefits.* New York: Penguin Classics, 1989.

Mankiw, N. Gregory. "Defending the One Percent," *Journal of Economic Perspectives* 27, no. 3 (2013): 21-24.

Mankiw, N. Gregory. "Response" (to Solow). *Journal of Economic Perspectives* 28, no. 1 (2014): 244-245.

Maskin, Eric. "Where do we go from here?" Arrow Lecture, Columbia University, December 11, 2009.

Mill, John Stuart. *Principles of Political Economy with Some of their Applications to Social Philosophy.* Middlesex, England: Penguin Books, 1970.

Mill, John Stuart. *On Liberty*. Indianapolis: Hackett, 1978.

Mises, Ludwig. *Socialism: an Economic and Sociological Analysis*. 6th Ed. New Haven: Yale University Press, 1951. Published first in German, 1922.

Myrdal, Gunnar. *The Political Element in the Development of Economic Theory*. London: Routledge, 1953. Published first in German, 1930.

Myrdal, Gunnar. *Beyond the Welfare State, economic planning and its international implications*. New Haven: Yale University Press, 1960.

National Academy of Sciences Committee on Prospering in the Global Economy of the 21st Century. *Rising Above the Gathering Storm: Energizing and Employing America for a Brighter Economic Future*. Washington, DC: The National Academies Press, 2007.

Nozik, Robert. *Anarchy, The State, and Utopia*. New York: Basic Books, 1974.

Nussbaum, Martha. *Creating Capacities: The Human Development Approach*. Cambridge, Massachusetts: Belknap, 2011.

Okun, Arthur. *Equality and Efficiency*. Washington, DC: Brookings, 1975.

Piel, Gerhard (1997). "Urbanization of Poverty Worldwide." *Challenge* 40, no. 1 (1997): 58-68.

Piketty, Thomas. *Capital in the Twenty-First Century*. Trans. By Arthur Goldhammer. Cambridge, Massachusetts: Belknap Press, 2014.

Pomeranz, Kenneth. *The Great Divergence: China, Europe, and the Making of the Modern World Economy*. Princeton: Princeton University Press, 2000.

Pope Francis. *Evangelii Gaudium*. Rome: Vatican Press, 2013.

Posner, Eric. "Human Welfare, Not Human Rights." *Columbia Law Review* 108 (2008): 1758-1801.

Puska, Pekka. "Successful prevention of non-communicable diseases: 25 year experiences with North Karelia Project in Finland." *Public Health Medicine* 4, no. 1 (2002): 5-7.

Rawls, John. *A Theory of Justice.* Cambridge: Harvard University Press, 1971.

Robinson, Joan. *Economic Philosophy.* New York: Anchor Books edition, 1964.

Rosenthal, Howard. "Why Hasn't Democracy Slowed Rising Inequality?" *Journal of Economic Perspectives* 27, no. 3 (2013): 237-283.

Sachs, Jeffrey. *Poland's Jump to the Market System.* Cambridge: MIT, 1993.

Schultze, Charles. *The Public Use of Private Interest.* Washington, DC: Brookings, 1976.

Schumpeter, Joseph. *Capitalism, Socialism, and Democracy.* Perennial Modern Thought Edition. New York: Harper, 2008.

Sen, Amartya. *Commodities and Capabilities.* Amsterdam: North-Holland, 1958.

Sen, Amartya. *Nobel lecture,* December 8, 1998. Also published in the *American Economic Review* 89, no. 3 (1999): 349-378.

Sen, Amartya. *Development as Freedom.* New York: Anchor Books, 1999.

Sinclair, Upton. *The Jungle.* New York: Doubleday, 1906.

Smith, Adam. *Theory of Moral Sentiments.* London: A. Millar, 1790.

Smith, Adam. *An Inquiry into the Nature and Causes of the Wealth of Nations.* London: Methuen & Co., Ltd., 1904.

Soderlind, Steven. "Particularly Polar Programs: Social Economics and Divergent Settlement Policies in Postwar Scandinavia." *Review of Social Economy* 70, no. 4 (2012): 164-180.

Solow, Robert. "The One Percent," *Journal of Economic Perspectives* 28, no. 1 (2014): 243-244.

Solzhenitsyn, Aleksander. *One Day in Life of Ivan Denisovich.* New York: Bantam Books, 1963.

Solzhenitsyn, Aleksander. *The Gulag Archipelago.* New York: Harper and Row, 1973.

Steinbeck, John. *Grapes of Wrath.* New York: Viking Press, 1939.

Stern, Nicolas. *The Economics of Climate Change.* Cambridge: Cambridge University Press, 2007.

Stiglitz, Joseph, Sen, Amartya, and Fitousi, Jean-Paul. *Mismeasuring Our Lives: Why GDP Doesn't Add Up.* New York: The New Press, 2010. This is essentially a reprint of the *Report by the Commission on the Measurement of Economic Performance and Social Progress,* 2009, requested by French President Sarkozy.

Thaler, Richard and Sunstein, Cass. "Libertarian Paternalism is Not an Oxymoron." *University of Chicago Law Review* 70, no. 4 (2003): 1159-1202.

Tiebout, Charles. "A Pure Theory of Public Expenditures." *Journal of Political Economy* 64, no. 5 (1956): 416-24.

Veblen, Thorstein. *The Theory of the Leisure Class: An Economic Study of Institutions.* New York: Dover, 1994.